Florence's
25Best

by Susannah Perry

Fodor's Travel Publications
New York • Toronto • London • Sydney • Auckland
www.fodors.com

How to Use This Book

KEY TO SYMBOLS

✚ Map reference to the accompanying fold–out map

✉ Address

☎ Telephone number

③ Opening/closing times

🍴 Restaurant or café

🚆 Nearest rail station

Ⓜ Nearest subway (Metro) station

🚌 Nearest bus route

⛴ Nearest riverboat or ferry stop

♿ Facilities for visitors with disabilities

❓ Other practical information

▷ Further information

ℹ Tourist information

✋ Admission charges: Expensive (over €5), Moderate (€3–€5), and Inexpensive (under €3)

★ Major Sight   ★ Minor Sight

👣 Walks   🚍 Excursions

🎫 Shops

🎵 Entertainment and Nightlife

🍴 Restaurants

This guide is divided into four sections

• **Essential Florence**: An introduction to the city and tips on making the most of your stay.

• **Florence by Area**: We've broken the city into four areas, and recommended the best sights, shops, entertainment venues, nightlife and restaurants in each one. Suggested walks help you to explore on foot.

• **Where to Stay**: The best hotels, whether you're looking for luxury, budget or something in between.

• **Need to Know**: The info you need to make your trip run smoothly, including getting about by public transport, weather tips, emergency phone numbers and useful websites.

Navigation In the Florence by Area chapter, we've given each area its own colour, which is also used on the locator maps throughout the book and the map on the inside front cover.

Maps The fold-out map accompanying this book is a comprehensive street plan of Florence. The grid on this fold-out map is the same as the grid on the locator maps within the book. We've given grid references within the book for each sight and listing.

Contents

CONTENTS

Introducing Florence

Florence, the Cradle of the Renaissance: This little city contributes so much to European culture through its paintings, harmonious *palazzi* that line the narrow streets, monumental civic buildings and splendid churches dominating spacious piazzas.

Getting around is easy. The core of the city is tiny and you can walk nearly everywhere, made more pleasant with the pedestrianization of the area from the Duomo south through Piazza della Signoria to the Ponte Vecchio and east from the Signoria to Santa Croce. However, the sheer number of tourists during peak times can make walking slow. Yet Florentines have no intention of killing the goose that lays the golden egg, and have poured money into doing whatever's possible to make the city visitor-friendly. Prices are high, but not too high. Hotels and restaurants provide what their customers want; museums have been revamped wherever possible; and shopping is taken seriously.

Florence should be a pleasure, not a cultural marathon. Try to concentrate on what you want to do, not what you think you should do. You might find more pleasure in exploring the quiet streets of the Oltrarno, with little workshops, than standing in line for hours to jostle for two minutes in front of a Botticelli masterpiece. A picnic in the greenery of the Boboli Gardens may be more memorable than an overpriced pizza in a crowded bar. If you do want to saturate yourself with Renaissance art, plan ahead and reserve tickets.

Close to the city lies some of Italy's most beautiful countryside, a dreamy landscape of rolling hills dotted with villages and solitary cypresses. Even though every year sees a rise in visitors, the heart of Florence retains the richness of its golden age and little has changed since the great construction works of the Renaissance. But it's up to you to get beneath the crowded surface of Florence to the beautiful heart below.

Facts + Figures

- Florence attracts around 6 million visitors a year.
- The native population is around 370,000.
- Florence has one of the lowest birth rates in Italy.
- The Uffizi Gallery is Italy's most visited museum—some 1.6 million visitors a year.

UFFIZI BOMBING

In May 1993 a huge bomb exploded on the west side of the Uffizi, killing five people, causing structural harm to the building, destroying the Gregoriophilus Library and damaging some 32 pictures, three of which were totally destroyed. Once thought to have been the work of the Mafia, the crime remains unsolved and the culprits have never been caught.

ON THE BALL

The Medici family, virtual sovereigns from the 14th to 18th centuries, left their mark on every building owned by or connected with them, so look out for their coat of arms, a varying number of balls *(palle)* on a shield, on buildings everywhere. The *palle* probably represent pills or coins, references to their original trade as apothecaries and later their role as bankers.

FLOOD FACTS

In November 1966 the River Arno burst its banks to disastrous effect: The tide, bludgeoning through the streets reached as high as 6m (20ft) in the Santa Croce region. This was not the only flood there has ever been, however: Bridges were swept away in 1269 and 1333, and the city was submerged in 1557 and 1884, but not as badly as in 1966.

A Short Stay in Florence

DAY 1

Morning Make an early start and head to the **Duomo** (▷ 58–59) to gaze on its mighty proportions; alongside are the superb **Campanile** (▷ 56) and **Battistero** (▷ 55). You can find out more about the history at the nearby **Museo dell'Opera del Duomo** (▷ 62). If you are feeling fit climb to the top of either the Duomo or Campanile for great views of the city but remember you will probably be jostling for space.

Mid-morning Take a coffee at one of the café-terraces along the traffic-free Piazza del Duomo to recharge your batteries. Head northwest up to the **Mercato Centrale** (▷ 68) at San Lorenzo and check out the amazing fresh produce. You can then browse the leather stalls of the **Mercato San Lorenzo** (▷ 68)—keep a look out for pickpockets, make sure you're buying a bargain and don't be afraid to haggle.

Lunch Right by the market is the unassuming **Gozzi Sergio** (▷ 75), renowned for its hearty Tuscan fare.

Afternoon Finish your shopping and then walk down Via Pucci and right into Via Ricasoli—or take bus 1, 6 or 17—to the **Galleria dell'Accademia** (▷ 60–61) to view Michelangelo's massive masterpiece *David*. There's plenty more to see in the gallery, or you may prefer to visit nearby **San Marco** (▷ 65) before returning to your hotel.

Dinner For a special treat try **Hostaria Bibendum** (▷ 49) in the **Helvetia & Bristol** hotel in Via dei Pescioni (▷ 112). For a cheaper option there's **Belle Donne** (▷ 47), located close to **Via de' Tornabuoni** (▷ 36).

Evening Stroll down to the grandiose **Piazza della Repubblica** (▷ 39) with its triumphal arch, for a touch of Florentine atmosphere.

DAY 2

Morning Lines form from as early as 7am at the **Galleria degli Uffizi** (▷ 28–29), with its priceless paintings and sculptures, so get there as early as you can; be patient and you will be rewarded.

Mid-morning Just behind the Uffizi, relax with a coffee at **Rivoire** (▷ 50), the best and probably the most expensive café in **Piazza della Signoria** (▷ 32). Leave the piazza and turn left into Via Por Santa Maria and stroll over the **Ponte Vecchio** (▷ 34–35) to be dazzled by its jewellery shops. There are plenty more gift shops just over the bridge.

Lunch Grab a light lunch at the **Caffè Pitti** (▷ 91) opposite the entrance of the Palazzo Pitti.

Afternoon Take in the **Palazzo Pitti** (▷ 84–85). There are four museums, plus the Royal Apartments to see, or if the weather is hot you might choose to stroll in the **Boboli Gardens** (▷ 82). Be prepared for crowds. Then wander around the streets of Oltrarno and along to the church of Santa Maria del Carmine with the Cappella Brancacci and its wonderful frescoes. This area has workshops, local shops and cafes. If you are feeling fit cross over the bridge and walk along the riverfront to **Santa Croce** (▷ 33).

Dinner The **Boccadama** (▷ 47) wine bar-cum-restaurant is in a nice spot to appreciate the lively square of Santa Croce.

Evening If the weather is kind you can get a great view of the city after dark from **Piazzale Michelangelo** (▷ 87) in the southeast of Oltrarno. Catch bus 13 to get there. Alternatively, take bus 7 up to the hill town of **Fiesole** (▷ 97) for wonderful views of Florence illuminated at night.

Top 25

►►►

ESSENTIAL FLORENCE TOP 25

Bargello ▷ 24–25
Overview of Florentine sculpture through works by Michelangelo, and others.

Battistero ▷ 55 One of Florence's oldest buildings, famous for its three sets of bronze doors.

Campanile ▷ 56 An incredible sight towering 85m (278ft) over the city, and offering great views.

Via de' Tornabuoni ▷ 36
The cream of world fashion is elegantly displayed on this street in the heart of medieval Florence.

Santissima Annunziata ▷ 67 Elegant, neoclassical arches grace the facade of this lovely church built by Michelozzo.

Santa Maria Novella ▷ 66 A great Florentine church full of superb art-works.

Santa Croce ▷ 33 The largest Franciscan church in Italy incorporating the Cappella dei Pazzi. Gallileo and Michaelangelo are buried here.

San Miniato al Monte ▷ 83 A fine Romanesque church perched on a hill with wonderful views.

San Marco ▷ 65
Beautiful convent where the paintings of Fra Angelico are a feast for the eyes.

San Lorenzo ▷ 64 This church is a superb example of archetypal Renaissance architecture.

Ponte Vecchio ▷ 34–35
One of the immediately recognizable emblems of Florence.

Piazza della Signoria ▷ 32 A traffic-free sculpture gallery with elegant cafes and restaurants.

8

These pages are a quick guide to the Top 25, which are described in more detail later. Here they are listed alphabetically and the tinted background shows the area they are in.

Cappella Brancacci ▷ 80
The chapel is covered from top to bottom with a monumental fresco cycle.

Cappella dei Pazzi ▷ 26
An early Renaissance masterpiece by Filippo Brunelleschi.

Cappelle Medicee ▷ 57 ▼▼▼
The Medici family's private chapels, visable proof of the dynasty's wealth.

Duomo ▷ 58–59 A sublime masterpiece of Renaissance architecture with a mighty dome.

Fiesole ▷ 97 The perfect hilltop destination for a change from the city and its crowds.

Galleria degli Uffizi ▷ 28–29 One of Europe's oldest galleries to view Renaissance art.

Galleria dell'Accademia ▷ 60–61 Home to *David*, Michelangelo's world-famous sculpture.

Giardino di Boboli ▷ 82 A green space in the middle of Florence, a cool oasis on a hot summer's day.

Museo dell'Opera del Duomo ▷ 62 Home to the Duomo collection.

Museo di Storia della Scienza ▷ 27 The history of science brought to life with this fine collection.

Palazzo Vecchio ▷ 30
The grand embodiment of Florentine civic purposes from the 14th century.

Palazzo Pitti ▷ 84–85
The city's largest and most opulent palace containing a fine picture collection.

Palazzo Medici-Riccardi ▷ 63 A massive palace, the residence of the Medici until 1540.

Map labels:
Museo Stibbert
Giardino dei Semplici
San Marco
Giardino della Gherardesca
Santissima Annunziata
Cimitero degli Inglesi
Galleria dell'Accademia
Museo dell'Opera del Duomo
CAMPO DI MARTE
Bargello
SOUTH CENTRO 20–50
Santa Croce
Cappella dei Pazzi
SANTA CROCE
Arno
SAN NICCOLÒ
Camping Michelangelo
RICORBOLI
GAVINANA
San Miniato al Monte
Cimitero delle Porte Sante
BANDINO

◀ ◀ ◀

Shopping

Florence is high on every visiting shopper's itinerary, but it's also a big attraction for Italians, who rate it highly for leather goods, fabrics, bed linens, lingerie, china and ceramics. As Tuscany's capital, Florence has the pick of Tuscan goods and shops, and people come from all over the region for a wider choice than they'll find at home. In the era of the global market, much of what's on sale is available worldwide, but the choice is wider and the prices often lower for many Italian essentials. Designer fashion also draws the crowds; one of Florence's many claims to fame is as the headquarters of Gucci (▷ 42).

Something to Take Home

The nicest souvenirs are often everyday items—kitchenware, household linens, tools and quirky stationery. Head for the markets for good value espresso coffee-makers and the tiny cups to go with them, wonderful gadgets such as fish-scalers and plastic goods in vivid shades. Fresh produce and leather goods are also in plentiful supply in Florence's markets. Plastic also features heavily in the inexpensive and cheerful children's toys; best values are often in tiny shops away from the main streets. Food is a popular take-home; you could consider more prosaic goods than expensive

---

STREET TRADE

Street trading is an essential part of the Florentine scene, with tourists being offered everything from fake designer bags to lighters and African objects. Some traders are unlicensed and keep a constant eye open for approaching *carabinieri*, ready to scoop up their merchandise and run. The authorities are now clamping down on such practices. Red signs warning you to watch what you buy and beware of fakes are prominently displayed in central Florence. Throughout Italy purchases of counterfeited goods are punishable by law with fines of up to €10,000, and a policy of zero tolerance has been implemented. You have been warned!

Florence is the place to shop for shoes, designer names, culinary delights and toys

oils and wine—how about herb packs specially blended for different foods, the excellent stock cubes known as *dadi* or sachets of vanilla sugar?

Traditional Crafts
One of Florence's major attractions is the wealth of artisan workshops, clustered mainly across the river in the Oltrarno area. Many specialize in antiques restoration for the city's numerous dealers, but there's more. Look for picture framers where you can get new purchases mounted, shoemakers selling wonderful velvet pads and brushes and marble-paper makers where you may have a chance to watch the whole creative process.

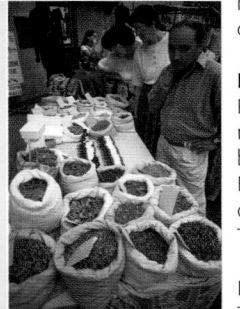

Florence on View
Prints, books and old maps and city plans make special souvenirs, and there are cookbooks on Tuscan cuisine, many in English. Beautiful calendars with views of Florence are on sale as early as April for the following year. The museum shops are good for these, too.

Florentine Kitsch
There's no chance that you'll be overwhelmed by good taste either; there are T-shirts bearing images of Michelangelo and Botticelli, plastic models of the Duomo and Ponte Vecchio, umbrellas shaped like the Duomo, grotesque ceramics and fakes of every description. Where else could you buy such a blatant silvery reproduction of Michelangelo's *David*, complete with twinkling lights?

Something to take home—a bag from the market, herbs, or a fashionable accessory from a top Florentine name

---

ON A BUDGET

Markets are the best source of inexpensive and second-hand clothing with an Italian twist. The weekly Cascine market (▷ 98) is where Florentines go for bargains—dive into the most crowded stalls. The area around San Lorenzo is good trawling ground for up-to-the-minute, inexpensive designs. The Mall (☎ 055 865 7775; www.themall.it), a 30-minute drive south of Florence at Leccio, has outlets for all the major top brands.

Shopping by Theme

For a more detailed write-up of these shops, see Florence by Area.

ANTIQUES/PRINTS

Antichità Monna Agnese (▷ 102)
Baccani (▷ 41)
Bartolozzi & Maioli (▷ 89)
Bottega delle Stampe (▷ 89)
La Casa della Stampa (▷ 89)
Cornici Campani (▷ 71)
Ducci (▷ 42)
Giovanni Turchi (▷ 90)
Vanda Nencioni (▷ 44)

CERAMICS/PORCELAIN

Armando Poggi (▷ 41)
Arte Creta (▷ 71)
Bartolini (▷ 71)
La Botteghina (▷ 71)
Ceramiche Artishiche Santa
    Caterina (▷ 102)
Ceramiche di Sugarò (▷ 101)
Ceramisti d'Arté (▷ 101)
Galleria Ponte Vecchio (▷ 89)
Lenzi Ghino Giacomo (▷ 101)
Pampaloni (▷ 43)
Richard Ginori (▷ 73)
Sbigoli Terrecotte (▷ 73)

FASHION

Angela Caputi (▷ 41)
Anna (▷ 89)
Blunauta (▷ 71)
Coin (▷ 41)
Cortecci Abbigliamento
    (▷ 102)
Echo (▷ 72)
Emilio Cavallini (▷ 42)
Emilio Pucci (▷ 42)
Gucci (▷ 42)
Hermès (▷ 72)
Intimissimi (▷ 72)
J. T. Casini (▷ 90)
Luisa Via Roma (▷ 43)

Max & Co (▷ 43)
MaxMara (▷ 72)
Pitti Boutique (▷ 90)
Prada–Donna (▷ 44)
Raspini (▷ 73)
La Rinascente (▷ 44)
Roberto Cavalli (▷ 44)
Sisley (▷ 44)
Tessuti A Mano (▷ 102)

GOLD/JEWELLERY

Alcozer & J (▷ 89)
Bottega Orafa Penko (▷ 71)
Cassetti (▷ 41)
Fratelli Piccini (▷ 42)
The Gold Corner (▷ 42)
Ornamenta (▷ 72)
Parenti (▷ 43)

LEATHER/SHOES

A. Risaliti (▷ 41)
Il Bosonte (▷ 41)
Cellerini (▷ 41)
Fratelli Rossetti (▷ 42)
Furla (▷ 42)
Leather School (▷ 42)
Madova Gloves (▷ 90)
Martelli (▷ 43)
Misuri (▷ 43)
Rive Gauche (▷ 90)
Romano (▷ 44)
Salvatore Ferragamo (▷ 44)

LINEN/FABRICS

Antico Setificio Fiorentino
    (▷ 89)
Ermeni (▷ 72)
Frette (▷ 72)
Loretta Caponi (▷ 72)
Siena Ricama (▷ 102)
Valmar (▷ 44)

PHARMACISTS

Farmacia Molteni (▷ 42)
Farmacia Pitti (▷ 89)

STATIONERY/GIFTS

Abacus (▷ 71)
Alice's Masks Art Studio (▷ 71)
Bottega del Mosaico (▷ 89)
Fratelli Alinari (▷ 72)
Giulio Giannini e Figlio (▷ 90)
Letizia Fiorini (▷ 42)
Libreria Antiquaria Gonnelli
    (▷ 72)
Moleria Locchi (▷ 90)
Olfattorio (▷ 43)
Il Papiro (▷ 73)
Parione (▷ 43)
Le Pietre Nell'Arte (▷ 73)
Pineider (▷ 44)
Scriptorium (▷ 73)
Il Torchio (▷ 90)

WINE/FOOD

Arte del Cioccolato (▷ 41)
Borgo (▷ 71)
La Bottega della Frutta (▷ 41)
Caniparoli (▷ 101)
Casa del Vino (▷ 71)
Drogheria Manganelli (▷ 102)
Federico Salza (▷ 101)
Marsili Costantino (▷ 101)
Morbidi (▷ 102)
Olio & Convivium (▷ 90)
Osteria de l'Ortolano (▷ 72)
Pegna (▷ 43)
Per Bacco (▷ 43)
Taddeucci (▷ 101)
Terre dei Gigli (▷ 73)
Vinarius (▷ 44)
Zanobini (▷ 73)

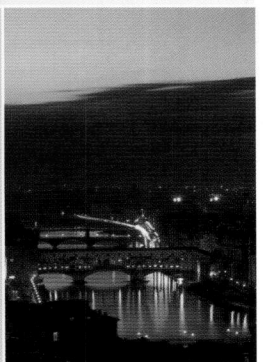

Florence by Night

To kick off your evening and for a taste of local life don't miss the *passeggiata*. Year-round, this quintessentially Italian nightly ritual sees the streets thronged with hundreds of locals, out to see and be seen, while window-shopping and meeting friends.

An Evening Stroll
The best place to see the fashion peacocks in their finery is on Via dei Calzaiuoli, linking Piazza del Duomo with Piazza della Signoria. To enjoy a drink while you people-watch, go to Piazza della Repubblica, with its expensive cafes. After dinner, wander along the Lungarni, the name given to the streets beside the river. The Ponte Vecchio is just as crowded by night as by day.

Stunning by Night
Evening is the ideal time to admire Florentine architecture as the floodlighting enhances many buildings. Don't miss the Piazza della Signoria and the area between it and the Duomo. The private *palazzi* look superb at this time of day and you can peek into courtyards and loggias. Street entertainers add to the atmosphere.

Culture, Concerts and Clubbing
Florence has a year-round schedule of cultural evening events. The free monthly tourist magazine *Chiavi d'Oro Toscana* has full listings. Newspapers are another good source. *Firenze Spettacolo* also details everything that's on including rock concerts, clubs and discos.

A night out? Choose from a walk by the river, a concert in a church, or a drink in one of the city's historic bars

---

PICK OF THE PANORAMAS

A great evening vantage point is Piazzale Michelangelo (▷ 87), which gives a glorious panorama of the Duomo illuminated, Florence's twinkling lights and the misty hills beyond. The square draws the crowds during the day but things are quieter at night. There's a restaurant and a couple of bars if you want to spend the evening here; avoid the park/gardens area below the square at night. In late June, the square hosts the spectacular fireworks display celebrating the feast of San Giovanni.

Eating Out

Eating is definitely one of life's pleasures in Florence, as it is all over Italy. The food is fresh, seasonal and, above all, local. You'll eat the best of Tuscan produce cooked to Tuscan recipes.

Mealtimes

If you are heading for breakfast in a bar, most open for business around 7–7.30. Restaurants normally open for lunch around 12.30 or 1 and stop serving at 3; they close for the afternoon and reopen for dinner around 7.30–8. The majority of restaurants have one closing day a week but many open every day in summer.

Where to Eat

Trattorie are usually family-run places and are generally more basic than restaurants. Sometimes there is no written menu and the waiter will reel off the list of the day's specials. They normally open for lunch and in the evening. *Ristoranti* are not always open for lunch. The food and surroundings are usually more refined than those of a trattoria. Both, however, add a cover charge, which includes bread, and a service charge to the bill. *Pizzerie* specialize in pizzas, but often serve simple pasta dishes as well. Look out for *forno al legno*—pizzas cooked in a wood-fired oven. *Osterie* can either be old-fashioned places specializing in home-cooked food or extremely elegant, long-established restaurants.

PAYING THE BILL

Pay by requesting the bill (*il conto*), and check to see whether service is included. Scribbled bills on scraps of paper are illegal; if you don't get a proper one, say that you need a receipt (*una recevuta*), which all restaurants, bars and shops are legally obliged to issue. Both they and you can be fined if you do not take this with you. Some smaller establishments expect to be paid in cash but you'll be able to use a credit card in most establishments. If service is included, it's customary to leave a small tip—some loose change will do.

Italian cuisine Florentine-style. It's morning coffee, ice cream, wine and pasta that will stay in the memory

Restaurants by Cuisine

There are restaurants to suit all tastes and budgets in Florence. On this page they are listed by cuisine. For a more detailed description of each restaurant, see Florence by Area.

COFFEE/PASTRIES

Caffé Amerini (▷ 47)
Caffé Pitti (▷ 91)
Cammillo (▷ 91)
Gilli (▷ 48)
Guibbe Rosse (▷ 48)
Paszkowski (▷ 50)
Rivoire (▷ 50)
Robiglio (▷ 76)

ELEGANT

Belcore (▷ 75)
Cantinetta Antinori
   (▷ 75)
Enoteca Pinchiorri (▷ 48)
La Giostra (▷ 75)
Hostaria Bibendum
   (▷ 49)
Incanto (▷ 49)
Orvm (▷ 49)
Relais le Jardin (▷ 76)
Ristorante San Michele
   (▷ 105)
Sabatini (▷ 76)

ICE CREAM

Gelateria Carabé (▷ 75)
Perché No! (▷ 50)
Vivoli (▷ 50)

INTERNATIONAL

Eito (▷ 48)
Kome (▷ 49)
Maracana Grill (▷ 92)

PIZZAS/SNACKS

Baldovino (▷ 47)
La Bussola (▷ 47)
Cantinetta dei Verrazzano
   (▷ 47)
Coquinarius (▷ 75)
Gusto Leo (▷ 49)
Procacci (▷ 50)
Le Volpi e l'Uva (▷ 92)

TUSCAN/FLORENTINE

Al Marsili (▷ 106)
Alle Murate (▷ 47)
Antico Barile (▷ 47)
Boccadama (▷ 47)
La Buca (▷ 106)
Buca di Sant Antonio
   (▷ 105)
Il Campo (▷ 106)
Il Cantinone (▷ 92)
La Casalinga (▷ 92)
Il Cibreo (▷ 48)
Coco Lezzone (▷ 48)
Da Benvenuto (▷ 48)
De Bruno (▷ 106)
La Decima Musa (▷ 48)
Dei Frescobaldi (▷ 48)
Gozzi Sergio (▷ 75)
Il Latini (▷ 49)
Le Mossacce (▷ 75)
Oliviero (▷ 49)
Osteria de' Benci (▷ 49)
Osteria del Cinghiale
   Bianco (▷ 92)
Osteria le Logge
   (▷ 106)

Osteria Machiavelli
   (▷ 105)
Pallottino (▷ 50)
Palle d'Oro (▷ 75)
Ristorante Beccofino
   (▷ 92)
Ristorante Il Fiesolano
   (▷ 105)
Ristorante I Polpa
   (▷ 105)
Rousseau il Doganiere
   (▷ 105)
Sotto le Fonti (▷ 106)
Taverna del Bronzino
   (▷ 76)
La Taverna di San
   Guiseppe (▷ 106)
Trattoria 13 Gobbi (▷ 50)
Trattoria Ponte Vecchio
   (▷ 50)
Trattoria Sant'Agostino 23
   (▷ 92)
Zà-Zà (▷ 76)

VEGETARIAN/ETHNIC

Al Tranvai (▷ 91)
Belle Donne (▷ 47)
Osteria Santo Spirito
   (▷ 92)
Ruth's (▷ 76)
Trattoria Antellesi (▷ 76)
Trattoria Antichi Cancelli
   (▷ 76)
Trattoria da Leo (▷ 105)
Trattoria Marione (▷ 50)

If You Like...

However you'd like to spend your time in Florence, these top suggestions should help you tailor your ideal visit. Each suggestion has a fuller write-up elsewhere in the book.

EXCLUSIVE SHOPPING

Descend on Via de' Tornabuoni (▷ 36) for the best in designer names—Armani, Gucci, Prada.
Sparkling gold and exquisite jewellery line either side of the Ponte Vecchio (▷ 34–35).
Florence is famed for its superb Italian shoes, and one of the best is Salvatore Ferragamo (▷ 44); you can visit the museum, too (▷ 38).

TAKING A SOUVENIR HOME

Stationery—Pineider (▷ 44) has the most gorgeous array of handmade paper and bound notebooks, plus pens and desk accessories.
Ceramics—choose an authentic jug or pot (▷ 89) from the large selection at the Galleria Ponte Vecchio.
Wine—all price ranges for the local Tuscan Chianti from Casa Del Vino (▷ 71).

If you want to capture the true essence of Florence try all things local and take something home

EATING LOCAL CUISINE

Sit at a shared table, trying out local dishes, at Belle Donne (▷ 47).
The cuisine is Tuscan, the restaurant fashionable—try Coco Lezzone (▷ 48) for that classic meal.
Close to the bridge of the same name, try Trattoria Ponte Vecchio (▷ 50).

HISTORIC CAFES

Gilli (▷ 48)—watch the world go by in the Piazza della Repubblica.
Paszkowski (▷ 50)—more indulgence on the Piazza della Reppublica—try the fruit tarts.
Rivoire (▷ 50)—set in the attractive Piazza Signoria, it's perfect to unwind in.

Italian ice cream at its best uses local produce and the freshest of ingredients

INDULGING IN ICE CREAM

You'll have difficulty deciding what to choose at Perché No! (▷ 50).

For delicious granitas and their special fruity *cremolata* visit Gelateria Carabé (▷ 75).

The most famous of all *gelateria* in Florence, Vivoli (▷ 50) changes its specials to suit the seasons.

A ROOM WITH A VIEW

Try the Hermitage (▷ 110) with its roof garden overlooking the River Arno.

For a panoramic bird's-eye view of the rooftops of Florence, try the bohemian Sorelle Bandini (▷ 109).

Some of the best views of the Tuscan countryside are from the hilltop town of Fiesole (▷ 97); for luxury as well try Villa San Michele (▷ 112).

SPLASHING OUT

Stay in the Helvetia & Bristol (▷ 112) for sheer luxury and elegance.

Shop in Via de' Tornabuoni (▷ 36) and stock your wardrobe with the top names in design.

Treat yourself to a refined cup of coffee at the stylish Paszkowski (▷ 50).

Stationery has been made for centuries (above); Italian fashion at its best (below)

PUTTING A SMILE ON THE KIDS' FACES

The Museo Stibbert (▷ 98) has a fine collection of armour for your budding knights.

Go to the soccer stadium (▷ 104) to cheer on local team Fiorentina when they're at home.

If you need to cool off, visit the Piscina le Pavoniere (▷ 104) outdoor pool.

FLORENCE ON A BUDGET

More delights of the city; ring the bell for a legendary cocktail

For good value combined with historic surroundings stay at the hotel Chiazza (▷ 109).
If the real thing is a bit pricey, there are some great look-a-like bargains at San Lorenzo market (▷ 68).
There's no charge to see the stunning paintings in the church of Santa Felicita (▷ 87).

THE CITY BY NIGHT

Sip a cocktail in the world-famous nightspot, Harry's Bar (▷ 46).
Take a trip up to Piazzale Michelangelo (▷ 87) to view the city in all its glory at night.
Attend a concert or opera at Florence's largest concert hall, Teatro Comunale. (▷ 74).

A LAZY MORNING

Relax over breakfast on the roof garden of a hotel such as the Hermitage (▷ 110).
Amble down to the Boboli Gardens (▷ 82), a cool oasis on a hot summer's day and just the spot for a picnic.
Take refuge in the calm and tranquillity of Santa Maria Maddelena dei Pazzi (▷ 69).

TO DO SOMETHING DIFFERENT

Try your luck on the horses at the Ippodromi Fiorentini (▷ 104). Trotting races take place here as well.
Hop on a bus and venture out to see some of Florence's interesting suburbs or lovely hill towns such as Fiesole (▷ 97).
Be uplifted at a recital in one of Florence's splendid churches such as Santa Maria de'Ricci (▷ 46).

There are plenty of green spaces in the city where you can relax

It doesn't take long to find a view in Florence, particularly from the top of a church such as San Miniato al Monte

Florence by Area

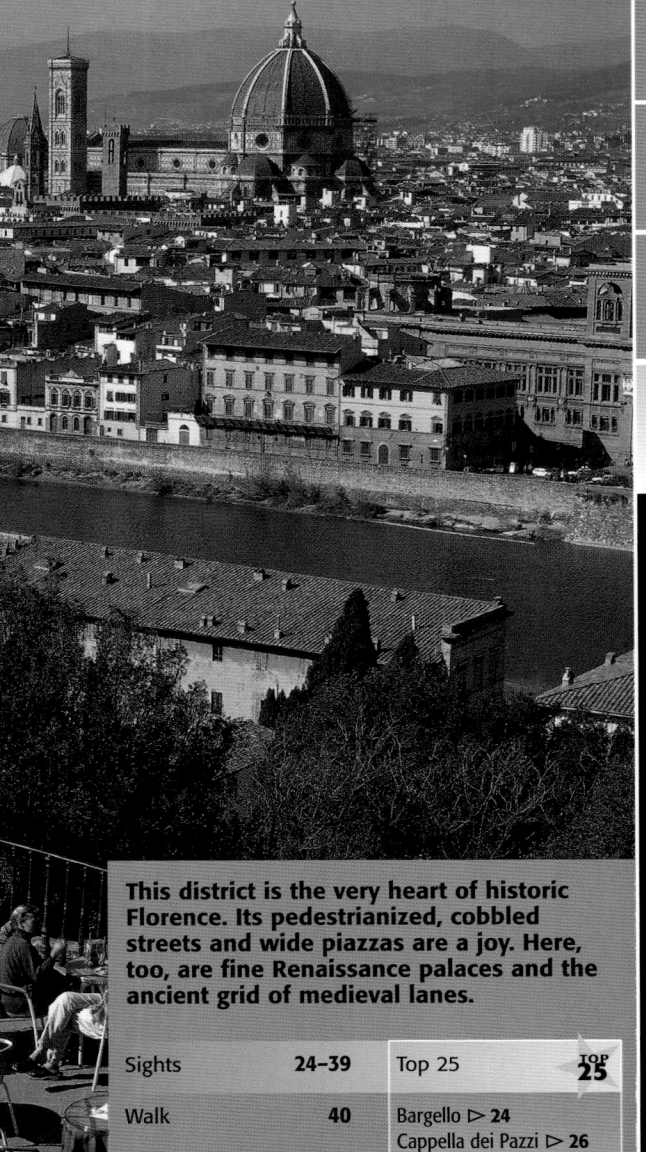

This district is the very heart of historic Florence. Its pedestrianized, cobbled streets and wide piazzas are a joy. Here, too, are fine Renaissance palaces and the ancient grid of medieval lanes.

3

4

5

IL PRATO
V.M Finiguerra
Via Montebello
Via Melegnano
VIA DELLA SCALA
Piazza
Santa Maria
Novella
VIA DE'
Ognissanti
BORGO
Palazzo
Lenzi
Ercole
Piazza
Ognissanti
Via dei
Porcellana
P
Palazzuolo
V. D
RONDINELLI
Via de' Trebbio
VIA DELLE BELLE DONNE
Via delle Belle Donne
Via delle Spada
Via del Sole
Ospedale di
San Giovanni
di Dio
Museo
Marino
Marini
TORNABUONI
Via dei
Via degli Agli
Via de' Pecori
Campidoglio
Via de' Banchi
**Piazza della
Repubblica**
Via dell' Oche
Via de' Calzaiuoli
**Casa di
Dante**

LUNGARNO
AMERICO
OGNISSANTI
VESPUCCI
PONTE
A VESPUCCI
Palazzo
Rucellai
Via d Vigna
Nuova
Palazzo
Goldoni
Via dei
LUNGARNO CORSINI
Palazzo
Corsini
**Via de'
Tornabuoni**
Via degli
Anselmi
Via della Spada
Piazza
Strozzi
Palazzo
Strozzi
Via della Vigna
Via della Monna
Via Porta
Rossa
Pellicceria
Via Calimala
Via degli
Strozzi
**San Martino
del Vescovo**
**Orsan-
michele**
**Badia
Fiorentina**
Via Dante
Alighieri
Piazza di
San
Firenze
Palazzo
Gondi
Via dei Proconsolo

6

PONTE ALLA
CARRAIA
Parione
Palazzo
**Santa
Trinita**
**Museo
Salvatore Ferragamo**
Colonna della Giustizia
Piazza di
Santa Trinita
**Ponte
Santa Trinita**
Palazzo
Davanzati
LUNGARNO ACCIAIUOLI
Via Por Santa
Maria
S Stefano
**Mercato
Nuovo**
Via Condotta
**Piazza
della Signoria**
Via dei
Santi
Apostoli
**Galleria
degli Uffizi**
**Museo di Storia
della Scienza**
LUNGARNO
ARCHIBUSIER
**Ponte
Vecchio**
I MEDICI
LUNGARNO
V Vinegia
**Palazzo
Vecchio**
Via dei Castellani
Palazzo
Vita
Piazza
Mentana
LUNGARNO GEN

Arno

7

8

0 _____ 250 m
0 _____ 250 yds

D   **E**   **F**

Palazzo
Alessandri
Palazzo del
Pandolfini
Borghese
Via
Bargello
Via Ghibellina
Via della Vigna Vecchia
Via dell'
Torta
San Firenze
Anguillara
Bgo de' Greci
Palazzo dei
Da Diacceto
Via dei Neri
Museo
Horne
DIAZ
Via
Teatro G
Verdi
Piazza
Santa Croce
Palazzo
dell'Antella
Borgo S Croce
Borgo s Croce
Trintori
Piazza dei
Cavalleggeri
LUNGARNO DELLE GRAZIE
PONTE ALLE
GRAZIE

GIUSEPPE VERDI
Via dei Martiri del
Popolo
Via Pietrapiana
Loggia del
Pesce
Sant'
Ambrogio
Borgo
la
Croce
Piazza
Cesare
Beccaria
Casa
Buonarroti
Via
Via Ghibellina
Ghibellina
Piazza
L Ghiberti
Marci
Mercato
Sant'Ambrogio
Porta alla
Croce
Carceri di
S Verdiana
dell'Agnolo
V.A Marton
Via
Via S Cristofano
Via delle
Conciatori
Borgo
Via di s Giuseppe
Casine
Via delle
Ghibellina
Carceri
d Murate
V le Duca
d Abruzzi
Santa
Croce
Largo
Piero Bargellini
Cappella
dei Pazzi
Via de'
Via Pietro Thouar
VIALE GIOVINE ITALIA
Biblioteca
Nazionale
SANTA CROCE
Via de' Malcontenti
Via
Tripoli
Torre delle
Zecca
Piazza
Plave
LUNGARNO DELLA ZECCA VECCHIA
LUNGARNO
PECORI GIRALDI

G   H   J

Bargello

HIGHLIGHTS

- Donatello's *David*
- Giambologna's *Mercury*
- Giambologna's animals
- Michelangelo's *Bacchus*
- Della Robbia's terracottas
- Courtyard

TIP

● The museum is very popular and in high season it is best to book in advance.

The Bargello, with its airy courtyard, is so pleasant that you would want to visit it even if it were not home to what is arguably the finest collection of Renaissance sculpture in the world.

Diverse uses Built in 1255, the Bargello was the first seat of Florence's city government and served as the city's main law court before being passed to the *Bargello* (Chief of Police) in 1574; it was used as a prison until 1859. In 1865 it opened as a museum, with an unrivalled collection of Renaissance sculpture and decorative arts.

Courtyard art The courtyard walls, once the site of executions, carry the coats of arms of the *Podestà* (chief magistrates), whose headquarters were here, and 16th-century sculpture, including

Clockwise from left: The Bargello viewed from the Campanile; inside the vaulted Bargello; the plaque of Christina de'Medici; bust of Piero di Lorenzo di Medici; the striking facade of the Bargello; stained-glass crest; courtyard of the Bargello

Giambologna's *Oceanus* from the Boboli Gardens (▷ 82). The ground floor has important works by Michelangelo, Cellini and Giambologna, including *Mercury* (1564).

Sculpture, medals and bronzes In the Salone del Consiglio Generale, a vaulted hall on the first floor that was once the courtroom, works by Donatello include his decidedly camp bronze *David* (c1430–40), dressed in long boots and a jaunty hat (the first freestanding nude since the Roman period), and his *St. George* (1416), sculpted for the exterior of Orsanmichele (▷ 39). On the second floor enamel terracottas by the della Robbia family include the bust of a boy by Andrea della Robbia. Note the displays of Italian medals and small Renaissance bronzes. The arms room has ivory-inlay saddles, guns and armour.

THE BASICS

www.polomuseale.firenze.it

✚ G6
✉ Via del Proconsolo 4
☎ 055 238 8606/055 294 883
🕐 Daily 8.15–2; closed 1st, 3rd, 5th Sun, 2nd, 4th Mon of month and 1 Jan, 1 May, 25 Dec
🚌 14, 23, A
♿ Good
💶 Moderate

Cappella dei Pazzi

TOP 25

Monochrome interior of the Cappella dei Pazzi (left); the serene cloisters and chapel (right)

THE BASICS

✚ H6
✉ Piazza Santa Croce
☎ 055 246 6105
🕐 Mon–Sat 9.30–5.30, Sun 1–5.30
🚍 14, 23, C
♿ Good
💰 Moderate; joint ticket with Santa Croce and Museo dell'Opera
❓ Access is through Santa Croce

HIGHLIGHTS

● Cappella dei Pazzi
● Cloister
● Roundels of the evangelists
● Cimabue's crucifix (13th century)
● Taddeo Gaddi's fresco (1333)
● Donatello's *St. Louis of Toulouse* (1424)
● Museo dell'Opera

In contrast to the adjacent church of Santa Croce, a key stop on the tourist circuit, the cloisters are not much visited. The solitude is perfect for appreciating their grace and harmony.

Convent building On the south side of Santa Croce are the buildings of a former convent. These include the Cappella dei Pazzi, one of the great architectural masterpieces of the early Renaissance, and a 14th-century refectory, which houses the Museo dell'Opera di Santa Croce. This is one of the lowest areas in Florence, and to the left of the Cappella dei Pazzi a plaque almost 6m (20ft) up shows the high point of the November 1966 floodwaters. The second cloister, a haven of calm, was designed by Filippo Brunelleschi.

The Pazzi Chapel The Cappella, which was commissioned as a chapter house by Andrea dei Pazzi and designed by Brunelleschi (*c*1430), is incorporated into the cloisters. This domed chapel is done in grey *pietra serena* (grey sandstone) against a white plaster background, embellished only by enamel terracotta roundels.

Small but beautiful The museum contains many important works, including a restored crucifix by Giovanni Cimabue. On the walls a huge fresco by Taddeo Gaddi shows the Last Supper, the Tree of Life, St. Louis of Toulouse, St. Francis, St. Benedict and Mary Magdalene washing Christ's feet. Prominent is the gilded bronze statue of *St. Louis of Toulouse* (1424), sculpted by Donatello.

Museo di Storia della Scienza

Here you'll find a fascinating collection of scientific instruments, a reminder that the Florentine Renaissance was not only an artistic movement, but also fostered the origins of modern science.

Pure science In the 14th-century, Palazzo Castellani, which now houses the Museum of the History of Science, contained a well-organized collection, which in large part belonged to the Medici Grand Dukes. In 1775 the Museum of Physics and Natural Sciences was opened and in 1929 the collection was moved to its current location. The galleries are on the first and second floors; the ground floor is the library of the Istituto di Storia della Scienza.

Galileo Galilei A sizeable is exhibition devoted to Galileo (1564–1642), Pisa-born but adopted by the Medici as the court mathematician. Some exhibits border on the hagiographic: His telescope is there, but also the middle finger of his right hand, preserved in a reliquary.

More exhibits The map room has a 16th-century map of the world by the Portuguese cartographer Lopo Homem, revealing the limit of European geographical knowledge at that time: Australasia is nowhere to be found and the tip of South America fades into blankness. It also has a collection of armillary spheres, used to divine the movements of the planets. On the second floor is a series of 18th-century wax and ceramic models of birth deformities, with hints for the doctor.

THE BASICS

www.imss.fi.it

⊞ F6

✉ Piazza dei Giudici 1

☎ 055 265 311 or 055 293 493 (automated information)

🕐 Oct–end May Mon, Wed–Sat 9.30–5, Tue 9.30–1, (2nd Sun each month 10–1); Jun–end Sep Mon, Wed, Thu, Fri 9.30–5, Tue, Sat 9.30–1 (last admission 30 min before closing)

🚌 23

♿ Excellent

💰 Moderate

❓ Excellent guide book

HIGHLIGHTS

● Galileo's telescope
● Lopo Homem's map of the world (16th century)
● Antonio Santucci's armillary sphere (1573)
● Copy of Lorenzo della Volpaia's clock of the planets (1593)

THE SOUTH CENTRO

TOP 25

HIGHLIGHTS

- The Tribune (room 18)
- Giotto's *Ognissanti Madonna* (1310)
- Botticelli's *Birth of Venus* (1485) and *Primavera* (c1480)
- Piero della Francesca's *Federico da Montefeltro and Battista Sforza* (1460)
- Leonardo's *Annunciation* (1472–75) and *Adoration of the Magi* (1481)
- Michelangelo's *Holy Family* (1508)
- Titian's *Venus of Urbino* (1538)

TIPS

- Reserve in advance; waiting can be up to 3 hours.
- Plan what you want to see as backtracking is difficult.
- Be patient, highlights are often blocked by large groups.
- There are frequent long waits for the toilet, go before you arrive.

The Uffizi encompasses the artistic developments of the Renaissance and beyond. It is a powerful expression of Florence's extraordinary role in the history of art.

Medici art The gallery contains part of the Medici's art collection, bequeathed in 1737 by Anna Maria Luisa. The building was designed by Vasari, in the 1560s, as the administrative offices (*uffizi*) of the Grand Duchy. Parts of the building and collection that were damaged by the 1993 bomb were restored and reopened in 1998.

From sculpture to painting Today people come for the paintings, but until the 19th century the attraction was sculpture (mostly now in the Bargello, ▷ 24). The collection is displayed in chronological order, starting with the first stirrings

Clockwise from left: Serene detail of the Madonna in the Uffizi; crowds gather outside the Uffizi; The Holy Family by Michelangelo; the gallery seen from the River Arno; on the Ponte Vecchio bridge linking to the Uffizi gallery; artisitic magnificence in the gallery

of the Renaissance in the 13th century and ending with works by Caravaggio, Rembrandt and Canaletto from the 17th and 18th centuries. Uccello's *Battle of San Romano* (1456) exemplifies the technical advances of the Renaissance, while Filippo Lippi's *Madonna and Child with Two Angels* (c1465) reveals the emotional focus typical of the period.

Venus Perhaps most fascinating is the Tribune, an octagonal chamber with a mother-of-pearl ceiling. In the middle is the Medici *Venus*, whose sensuous derrière earned her the reputation of the sexiest sculpture of the ancient world. Portraits include Bronzino's *Giovanni de Medici* (c1549), a smiling boy holding a goldfinch. The café provides a welcome pitstop and has superb views of Piazza della Signoria.

THE BASICS

www.uffizi.firenze.it

⊞ F6

✉ Loggiato degli Uffizi 6

☎ 055 238 8651 (reserve ahead to avoid lines by calling 055 294 833)

🕐 Tue–Sun 8.15–6.50 (last admission 45 min before closing); closed 1 Jan, 1 May, 25 Dec

🍽 Cafe

🚌 23, B

♿ Good

✋ Expensive

Palazzo Vecchio

TOP 25

The striking Palazzo Vecchio dominating the skyline has many intricate details within

With its fortresslike castellations and its commanding 95m (311ft) bell tower, the Palazzo Vecchio conveys a message of political power supported by solid military strength.

Town Hall The Palazzo Vecchio is still Florence's town hall, as it has been since its completion by Arnolfo di Cambio in 1302. It was substantially renovated for Duke Cosimo I, who made it his palace in 1540. It became known as the Palazzo Vecchio (Old Palace) when Cosimo transferred his court to the Palazzo Pitti. During the brief period when Florence was the capital of Italy (1865–71), it housed the Parliament and Foreign Ministry.

Assembly room The vast Salone dei Cinquecento is 53.5m by 22m (175ft by 72ft); 18m (59ft) high and was designed in the 1490s, during the era of the Florentine Republic, as the meeting place of the 500-strong ruling assembly. Vasari painted the military scenes of Florence's victory over Siena and Pisa (1563–65). The theme of Florence's might is underscored by Michelangelo's *Genius of Victory* (1533–34), as well as sculptures of the *Deeds of Hercules* by Vincenzo dei Rossi.

Loggia views On the second floor the Terrazza di Saturno is an open loggia with views to the hills. The Sala dei Gigli is decorated with gold *fleurs-de-lys* and houses Donatello's *Judith and Holofernes* (1456–60). The Sala delle Carte (Map Room), has a wonderful collection of globes and maps painted on leather, showing the world in 1563.

THE BASICS

F6
Piazza della Signoria
055 276 8224
Mon–Wed, Fri, Sun 9–7, Thu 9–2 (also late opening Mon, Fri in summer)
23, B
Good
Moderate; combined ticket with Cappella Brancacci, expensive

HIGHLIGHTS

- Sala delle Carte
- Sala dei Gigli
- Michelangelo's *Genius of Victory*
- Donatello's *Judith and Holofernes*
- View from the Terrazza di Saturno
- Salone dei Cinquecento

Piazza della Signoria

The Piazza Signoria is a gathering place—from protests to costumed parades

THE BASICS

+ F6
⊠ Piazza della Signoria
🚌 23, A, B
♿ Good

HIGHLIGHTS

- Loggia dei Lanzi (1376)
- Cellini's *Perseus* (1554)
- Giambologna's *Rape of the Sabine Women* (1583)
- Ammannati's *Neptune* (1575)
- Rivoire café
- Sorbi newspaper and postcard kiosk

Standing in the Piazza della Signoria in the shadow of the grim, forbidding Palazzo Vecchio, it is impossible to escape the sense of Florence's past political might.

Political piazza The Piazza della Signoria has been the hub of political life in Florence since the 14th century. It was the scene of great triumphs, such as the return of the Medici in 1530, but also of the Bonfire of the Vanities instigated by Savonarola, who was himself burned at the stake here in 1498, denounced as a heretic by the Inquisition.

Significant sculptures The sculptures here bristle with political connotations, many of them fiercely contradictory. Michelangelo's *David* (the original is in the Accademia) was placed outside the Palazzo Vecchio as a symbol of the Republic's defiance of the tyrannical Medici. The *Neptune* (1575), by Ammannati, celebrates the Medici's maritime ambitions, and Giambologna's statue of *Duke Cosimo I* (1595) the man who brought all of Tuscany under Medici military rule. The statue of Perseus holding Medusa's head, by Cellini (1554), is a stark reminder of what happened to those who crossed the Medici. The graceful Loggia dei Lanzi, which functions as an open-air sculpture gallery, was designed by Orcagna in 1376.

Postcard paradise Sorbi, the newspaper kiosk, has an unrivalled collection of postcards and newspapers, which you could enjoy over a drink in the Rivoire café (▷ 50).

Aerial view of Santa Croce (left); detail of frescoes by Giotto in Santa Croce (right)

TOP 25

Santa Croce

Despite its vast size and swarms of tourists, Santa Croce is personal and touchingly intimate, perhaps because of the sense that one somehow knows the people buried here.

Burial place Santa Croce, rebuilt for the Franciscan order in 1294 by Arnolfo di Cambio, is the burial place of the great and the good in Florence. Michelangelo is buried in Santa Croce, as are Rossini, Machiavelli and the Pisa-born Galileo Galilei, who was excommunicated during the Inquisition and was not allowed a Christian burial until 1737, 95 years after his death. There is also a memorial to Dante, whose sarcophagus is empty.

Anglophile The church exterior is covered with |a polychrome marble facade added in 1863 and paid for by the English benefactor Sir Francis Sloane. It looks over the Piazza Santa Croce, site of an annual football game in medieval costume.

Artistic riches The artistic wealth in Santa Croce is stunning; frescoes by Gaddi (1380) in the Cappella Maggiore tell the story of the holy cross ('Santa Croce') and beautiful frescoes by Giotto in the Bardi and Peruzzi chapels show scenes from the lives of St. Francis and St. John the Evangelist. Don't miss the memorial to 19th-century playwright Giovanni Battista Nicolini, left of the entrance facing the altar, said to have inspired the *Statue of Liberty*. Santa Croce was severely hit by flooding in 1966, and you can still see a tide mark showing far up on the pillars and walls.

THE BASICS

www.santacroce.firenze.it
⊞ H6
✉ Piazza Santa Croce
☎ 055 246 105
🕐 Mon–Sat 9.30–5.30, Sun 1–5.30; closed during services
🚌 14, 23, C
♿ Good
👉 Moderate; joint ticket with Cappella dei Pazzi and Museo dell'Opera

HIGHLIGHTS

● Giotto's frescoes (1320–25)
● Tombs of Michelangelo, Machiavelli, Galileo
● Painted wooden ceiling
● Donatello's *Annunciation* (1435)
● Polychrome marble facade (1863)
● Wooden crucifix by Donatello
● 14th-century windows

THE SOUTH CENTRO

TOP 25

Ponte Vecchio

TOP
25

THE SOUTH CENTRO TOP 25

HIGHLIGHTS

- Gold and jewellery shops
- Views of the Arno
- *Corridoio Vasariano* (1565)
- Bust of Cellini (1900)

TIP

- The sun sets directly downriver from the bridge, and the golden tones of the structure itself are magical on a good evening.

No visit to Florence is complete without a saunter down this bridge; lined with old shops jutting precariously over the water, it is difficult to believe you're on a proper bridge and not just strolling down a narrow street.

The test of time Near the Roman crossing, the Old Bridge was, until 1218, the only bridge across the Arno in Florence. The current bridge was rebuilt after a flood in 1345. During World War II, it was the only bridge the Germans did not destroy but they blocked access by demolishing the medieval buildings either side. On 4 November 1966 the bridge survived when the Arno burst its banks.

Private path When the Medici moved from the Palazzo Vecchio to the Palazzo Pitti, they decided

Clockwise from left: The vaulted arcades of the Ponte Vecchio were rebuilt by Michelozzo; gold has been sold on the Ponte Vecchio for centuries; detail of a section of the bridge; the Ponte Veccchio at dusk; bust of the sculptor, soldier and goldsmith Benvenuto Cellini guarding the bridge

they needed a connecting route from the Uffizi to the Palazzo Pitti on the other side of the river that enabled them to keep out of contact with their people. The result was Vasari's *Corridoio Vasariano*, built in 1565 on top of the buildings lining the bridge's eastern parapet.

Glitz Shops have been on the Ponte Vecchio since the 13th century: Initially all types—butchers and fishmongers and later tanners, whose industrial waste caused a pretty rank stench. In 1593, Medici Duke Ferdinand I decreed that only gold-smiths and jewellers be allowed on the bridge. When the shops close their wooden shutters it makes them look like suitcases. As one of the places that Florentines regularly come to for the *passeggiata*, it is also always full of Senegalese street vendors, hawking fake goods.

THE BASICS

✚ F6
🚌 B, D
♿ Good

Via de' Tornabuoni

History meets style on the smartest street in town

THE BASICS

➕ E5–E6
✉ Via de' Tornabuoni
🚌 6, 11, A, B
♿ Good

HIGHLIGHTS

● Sassetti Chapel frescoes in Santa Trinità
● Ferragamo Shoe Museum
● Designer shops
● Palazzo Strozzi
● 17th-century facade of San Gaetano

Florence maybe one of the world's richest cultural cities, but it's also a place for serious shopping. Fashionable Via de' Tornabuoni supports the top names in fashion, set among the stunning palaces.

Shopping in palaces Italy has always been synonymous with style, think Milan or Rome, but Florence contributes in its own way, too. The city hosted Italy's earliest fashion shows in the 1950s, and innovative designers made their fortunes within the city's medieval palaces here on Via de' Tornabuoni. Salvatore Ferragamo, the flagship store and shoe museum (▷ 38), can be found within the Palazzo Spini Feroni, one of the best preserved private medieval palaces in Florence; while Guccio Gucci picked this street—three generations ago—for his headquarters, which is still based at 73r Tornabuoni. You may be intent on a bargain but spare a moment to glance up at the facades and interiors of the imposing buildings.

Beyond the shops At the north end of the street is the stunning Palazzo Antinori (1465), next to the city's greatest baroque church San Gaetano (1648), a tranquil spot to escape the crowds. Halfway down is the impressive Palazzo Strozzi. At the end is Piazza Santa Trinità with its artistically rich church. Central to the square is the tall Column of Justice, brought from the Baths of Caracalla in Rome and given to Cosimo I in 1560 by Pope Pius IV. Just beyond here is the Santa Trinità Bridge (▷ 39) that links elegant Tornabuoni with Oltrarno on the south bank of the River Arno.

More to See

BADIA FIORENTINA

The Badia Fiorentina, the oldest monastery in Florence, was founded in AD978 by Willa, widow of Umberto, Margrave of Tuscany. It is best known in connection with Dante, who used to meet Beatrice here. Its magnificent bell tower is Gothic at the top and Romanesque at the base. Inside are two works: Filippino Lippi's *The Madonna Appearing to St. Bernard*, left of the entrance, and the tomb of Count Ugo, son of Willa and Umberto.

➕ G6 ✉ Piazza San Firenze, entrance in Via Dante Alighieri ☎ No phone 🕐 Restricted opening, consult tourist office 🚌 14, 23, A ♿ Impossible 💰 Free

CASA BUONARROTI

www.casabuonarroti.it

This house, which Michelangelo bought in 1508, is now a fascinating museum and gallery. Exhibits include the artist's earliest known work, the *Madonna della Scala* (c1491), a wood and wax model (the only one of its type) of a river god and a model of the facade for San Lorenzo never executed.

➕ H6 ✉ Via Ghibellina 70 ☎ 055 241 752 🚌 14, A 🕐 Wed–Mon 9.30–2. Guided tours can be reserved ♿ Poor 💰 Expensive

CASA DI DANTE

www.museocasadidante.it

The 13th-century House of Dante has been restored and contains material relating to the author's life and work.

➕ F6 ✉ Via Santa Margherita 1 ☎ 055 219 416 🕐 Apr–Sep daily 10–6; Oct–Mar Tue–Sun 10–5 🚌 14, 23, A ♿ None 💰 Moderate

MERCATO NUOVO

So-called to distinguish it from the Mercato Vecchio, which used to be on the site of today's Piazza della Repubblica, this market is famous for the brass boar with a well-stroked nose, *Il Porcellino*, which sometimes lends its name to the market. It is also known as the 'straw market', a reference to the straw hats once sold here.

➕ F6 ✉ Loggiato del Porcellino, Via Porta Rossa 🕐 Mid-Mar to end Oct daily 9–8; Nov to mid-Mar Tue–Sun 9–7.30 🚌 A ♿ Good (but crowded)

The ceiling of the Badia Fiorentina is decorated with beautiful 15th-century frescoes

A popular pig in the Mercato Nuovo

MERCATO DI SANT' AMBROGIO

After the Mercato Centrale, this is the second most important market for fresh produce in Florence. It attracts Florence's working population, is inexpensive and is pleasantly noisy.

✚ H6 ✉ Piazza Lorenzo Ghiberti 🕐 Mon–Sat 7–2 🚌 A ♿ Good

MUSEO HORNE

www.museohorne.it

This small museum, housed in Palazzo Corsi, owes its existence to the English art historian and collector Herbert Percy Horne (1864–1916). Horne bought the palazzo in 1904 for his interesting collection of paintings, furniture and sculpture. On his death, he left the palazzo and its contents to Italy.

✚ G7 ✉ Via de Benci 6 ☎ 055 244 661 🕐 Mon–Sat 9–1; closed hols 🚌 23, B, C ♿ None 💷 Moderate

MUSEO SALVATORE FERRAGAMO

www.salvatoreferragamo.it

Founded in 1995, this collection of 10,000 pairs of shoes by Ferragamo dates from his return from Hollywood to Florence in 1927 until his death in the 1960s. The collection highlights Ferragamo's choice of hues, his imaginative models and experimentation with materials. Many examples were created for celebrities.

✚ E6 ✉ Palazzo Spini Feroni, Via de' Tornabuoni 2 ☎ 055 336 0456 🕐 Mon– Sat 10–1, 2–6 🚌 6, 11, A, B ♿ Poor 💷 Moderate

OGNISSANTI

This was the parish church of the Vespucci family, and of Botticelli's family; he was buried here. In the second chapel on the right facing the altar is a fresco by Ghirlandaio, which is said to include Amerigo's portrait (the boy behind the Virgin). In the convent's *cenacolo* (refectory) there are more Ghirlandaio pieces—a *Last Supper* and *St. Jerome in his Study*—and Botticelli's *St. Augustine in his Study*.

✚ D5 ✉ Borgo Ognissanti 42 ☎ 055 239 8700 🕐 Daily 7–12.30, 4–8. *Last Supper* in convent Mon, Tue, Sat 9–12 🚌 B, D ♿ Poor 💷 Free

An emblem on the Church of the Ognissanti (left); magnificent 17th- and 18th-century frescoes adorn the ceiling and walls of the Ognissanti (right)

ORSANMICHELE

Built as a grain market in 1337, Orsanmichele became a church in 1380. The city's guilds commissioned some of the best artists to make statues of patron saints to sit in the canopied niches, and so created a permanent outdoor exhibition of 15th-century Florentine sculpture. These statues are being removed one by one for restoration and copies put in their place. Some of the original works are still there, including Lorenzo Ghiberti's bronzes of St. Matthew (1419–22). A museum opened here in 2009 (Monday only, 10–5).

✚ F6 ✉ Via dei Calzaiuoli ☎ 055 284 944 🕐 Tue–Sun 10–5 🚌 A ♿ Good ✋ Free

PIAZZA DELLA REPUBBLICA

This grandiose square in the middle of Florence, on the site of the old market, was built in the 1870s, when Florence briefly was the capital of Italy. Florentines are not fond of the square's architecture nor its crass neoclassical triumphal arch, but it is an unusually large open space, where you can breathe a little and let a child run free. All around are excellent grand cafés, if somewhat overpriced.

✚ F6 🚌 A ♿ Good

PONTE SANTA TRINITÀ

The finest of Florence's bridges dates back to 1252, although what you see today is a well-executed replica of Ammannati's bridge built in 1567 and destroyed by the Nazis in 1944. Ammannati was commissioned by Cosimo I and probably consulted Michelangelo in his designs. Lovely views of Florence, especially the Ponte Vecchio, are to be had from here.

✚ E6 ✉ Ponte Santa Trinità 🚌 6, 11, 36, 37, B, D ♿ Good ✋ Free

SAN MARTINO DEL VESCOVO

This tiny oratory is set right in the heart of medieval Florence. Don't miss the *lunette* frescoes on the upper walls.

✚ F6 ✉ Piazza San Martino, Via Dante Alighieri 🕐 Mon–Sat 10–12, 3–5 (closed Fri pm) 🚌 A ♿ Acceptable ✋ Free

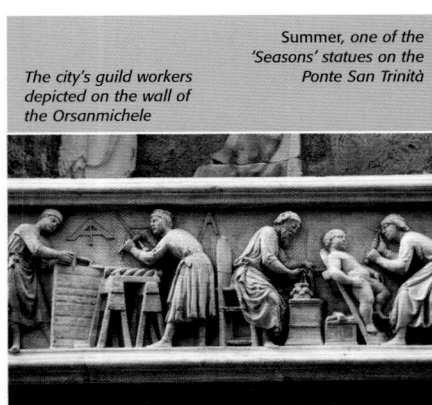

The city's guild workers depicted on the wall of the Orsanmichele

Summer, *one of the 'Seasons' statues on the Ponte San Trinità*

Dante's Florence

A short walk through the district where Dante lived, worked and played and on then to the eastern part of the city to Sante Croce.

DISTANCE: 1km (0.5 miles) approx **ALLOW:** 1 hour including visits

START

BATTISTERO (▷ 55)
✚ F5 🚌 1, 14, 23, A

END

SANTA CROCE (▷ 33)
✚ H6 🚌 14, 23, C

WALK

THE SOUTH CENTRO

1 Start at the Baptistery (▷ 55), where the poet Dante Alighieri was baptized. At that time, it was not covered with the marble facing that adorns the facade today.

2 According to tradition Dante watched the construction of the cathedral from the Sasso di Dante, a stone (marked) in the wall between Via dello Studio and Via del Proconsolo, opposite the Duomo.

3 Take Via dello Studio. Turn left at Via del Corso and take the first right onto Via di Santa Margherita. This leads to the Casa di Dante (▷ 37), one-time home of the author.

4 Opposite is San Martino del Vescovo (▷ 39), where Dante's family worshipped. Back toward Via del Corso is Santa Margherita, where his Beatrice went to Mass.

8 Dante's sarcophagus, inside the church, is empty. Despite all his connections with the city of Florence, Dante was buried in Ravenna.

7 Take the second left, Via dell'Anguillara, to reach Piazza Santa Croce. The streets are dotted with artisans' workshops. Outside the church of Santa Croce (▷ 33) there is a 19th-century statue of Dante.

6 Dante often saw Beatrice here and the Badia's bell would have punctuated Dante's daily life. Exit and turn onto Via del Proconsolo, past the Bargello (▷ 24–25), which was being built in Dante's time.

5 From Santa Margherita turn left onto Via Dante Alighieri for the entrance of the Badia (▷ 37).

Shopping

ANGELA CAPUTI

www.angelacaputi.com
Angela Caputi is the place
to look for bright, bold
and highly original cos-
tume jewellery. Clothing
and accessories to go
with the pendant or
earrings you have just
bought are also stocked.
➕ F6 ✉ Borgo Santi
Apostoli 44–46r ☎ 055 292
993 🚌 B

A. RISALITI

www.a-risaliti.com
'Risaliti' means a golden
guarantee, and that's
what you get at this
jewellers that oozes
class. Distinguished
clients, including Bette
Davis and Ava Gardner,
have admired their
beautiful handcrafted
pieces; gold with precious
stones in both classic
and modern designs.
➕ F6 ✉ Ponte Vecchio
27–29r ☎ 055 294 656
🚌 B, D

ARMANDO POGGI

www.apoggi.com
One of the widest selec-
tions of porcelain in the
city. Stocks Guiseppi
Armani figurines and
Richard Ginori porcelain.
➕ F5 ✉ Via Calzaiuoli 103r
and 116r ☎ 055 211 719 🚌 A

ARTE DEL CIOCCOLATO

www.artedelcioccolato.it
Chocolatier par excellence
Roberto Catinari learned
his craft in Switzerland
before returning to his
native Tuscany. His shop

is a shrine to the best in
chocolate-making–first-
class ingredients, superb
recipes and delicious
results.
➕ E6 ✉ Via Porta Rossi
(corner with Via de'
Tornabuoni) ☎ 055 217 136
🚌 6, 11, A

BACCANI

A beautiful shop, estab-
lished in 1903. The old
interior is filled with
prints, engravings, paintings and old maps. Prices
vary from very reasonable
to very expensive.
➕ D5 ✉ Borgo Ognissanti
22r ☎ 055 214 467 🚌 B, D

IL BISONTE

www.ilbisonte.net
With everything stamped
with the trademark bison,
this brand is at the cutting

GOLD FACTS

A dazzling array of gold is
for sale all over Florence,
most notably on the Ponte
Vecchio: In 1593 Ferdinand I
decreed that only goldsmiths
and jewellers should work
there and it has remained
that way ever since. The gold
sold in Florence is 18 carat,
often expressed as a rather
confusing 750 per cent (with
the per cent sign actually
referring to 1,000). Gold is
also found–at somewhat
lower prices–in the Santa
Croce area, where, in
accordance with tradition,
all gold jewellery and other
items are sold by weight.

edge of leather bags
and accessories.
➕ E6 ✉ Via del Panone 31r
☎ 055 215 772 🚌 6, 11, 36,
37, A, B

LA BOTTEGA DELLA FRUTTA

The owners search high
and low for more unusual
products for this family-
run business. The select
produce includes fresh
fruit, cheese, yogurts,
pasta, balsamic vinegar
and wine.
➕ E5 ✉ Via dei Federighi 31r
☎ 055 239 8590 🚌 6, A

CASSETTI

www.cassetti.it
Maria Grazia's collection
of quality jewellery,
including period items,
has attracted attention
from famous people such
as David Bowie, Bill
Clinton and Liz Taylor.
➕ F6 ✉ Ponte Vecchio
33–52–54r ☎ 055 239 6028
🚌 B, D

CELLERINI

www.cellerini.it
Elegant and sophisticated
leather bags of outstand-
ing quality. Styles tend to
be wonderfully simple yet
cleverly designed. Popular
among *fashionistas*.
➕ E5 ✉ Via del Sole 37r
☎ 055 282 533 🚌 36, 37, A

COIN

www.coin.it
A huge clothing and
design emporium with a
vast range of goods at
reasonable prices on the
Via dei Calzaiuoli. Open
on Sunday.

⊞ F5 ✉ Via dei Calzaiuoli
56r ☎ 055 280 531 🚇 A

DUCCI
www.duccishop.com
There is a huge selection
of tinted lithographs and
prints here, framed and
unframed. Some of the
unusual objets d'art
include wood carvings.
⊞ E6 ✉ Lungarno Corsini
24r ☎ 055 214 550 🚇 6,
11, 36, 37, B

EMILIO CAVALLINI
www.emiliocavallini.com
A wacky collection of
socks and hosiery.
⊞ E6 ✉ Via della Vigna
Nuova 24r ☎ 055 238 2789
🚇 6, A

EMILIO PUCCI
www.emiliopucci.com
A renowned Florentine
fashion house created in
1950 by Marquis Emilio
Pucci. This store on Via
de' Tornabuoni sells
fantastic, very pricey
separates, silk shirts,
shoes and accessories.
⊞ E6 ✉ Via de' Tornabuoni
20–22r ☎ 055 265 8082
🚇 6, 11, A

FARMACIA MOLTENI
www.farmacia-molteni.com
This historic pharmacy,
one of the oldest in
Florence, is open 24-
hours a day. It is worth a
visit to view the beautiful
interior alone, but in
addition it has a good
range of cosmetics and
natural products.
⊞ F5 ✉ Via dei Calzaiuoli 7r
☎ 055 215 472 🚇 A

FRATELLI PICCINI
www.fratellipiccini.com
If you go jewellery
shopping on the Ponte
Vecchio, make sure
you take in Piccini's.
They have lovely gold
charms, which make a
nice gift.
⊞ F6 ✉ Ponte Vecchio 23r
☎ 055 294 768 🚇 B, D

FRATELLI ROSSETTI
www.fratellirossetti.com
Beautifully crafted shoes
and boots in classic
Italian styles for men and
women.
⊞ F5 ✉ Piazza della
Repubblica 43–45r ☎ 055
216 656 🚇 A

FURLA
www.furla.com
Chic, handsomely
designed leather bags and
belts at prices that are less
astronomic than else-
where. There is another
branch of the store at Via
della Vigna Nouva 47.
⊞ F5 ✉ Via Calzaiuoli 47r
☎ 055 238 2883 🚇 A

THE GOLD CORNER
This frequent tour-group
stop in Piazza Sante
Croce sells gold by weight
along with typical Italian
cameos and coral.
⊞ G6 ✉ Piazza Santa Croce
15r ☎ 055 241 971 🚇 23, C

GUCCI
A predictably elegant and
pricey shop; headquarters
of the Gucci empire.
⊞ E6 ✉ Via de' Tornabuoni
73r ☎ 055 264 011 🚇 6,
11, 22, 36, 37, A

LEATHER SCHOOL
OF SANTA CROCE
www.scuoladelcuoio.com
At the back of the famous
church, off Via di San
Giuseppe, this workshop
was once run by
Franciscan monks and
sells quality craftsmanship
at the on-site shop.
⊞ G6 ✉ Via San Guiseppe
5r (off Piazza Santa Croce)
☎ 055 244 533 🚇 23, C

LETIZIA FIORINI
This beautiful little shop is
also the artist's workshop,
where she makes charm-
ing, and not expensive,
handcrafted puppets, dolls
and other toys. It's hard to

resist buying a Pinochio puppet or a jack-in-the-box to take home.

🔲 E6 ✉ Via del Parione 60r ☎ 055 216 504 🚌 6, A

LUISA VIA ROMA

www.luisaviaroma.com

A popular spot for Florence's image-conscious men and women. Eye-catching window displays conceal a sleek interior over two floors where well-known labels rub shoulders with Luisa's own designs.

🔲 F5 ✉ Via Roma 19–21r ☎ 055 906 4116 🚌 A

MARTELLI

www.martelligloves.it

This Florence institution has manufactured hand-made gloves since 1967. You would be hard pushed to find such an amazing selection elsewhere in every hue and fabric imaginable.

🔲 F6 ✉ Via Por Santa Maria 18r ☎ 055 239 6395 🚌 B

MAX & CO

The trendy branch of MaxMara sells well-designed high-fashion pieces to a mainly teenage clientele, plus a range of classics with a contemporary twist.

🔲 F5 ✉ Via dei Calzaiuoli 89r ☎ 055 288 656 🚌 A

MISURI

This is one of the best Santa Croce area leather factories.

🔲 G6 ✉ Piazza Santa Croce 20r ☎ 055 240 995 🚌 23, C

OLFATTORIO

www.olfattorio.it

Even if you don't want to buy, take a look at the striking display and interior of this perfumery. Let an expert find the fragrance to suit you, most of which are hand-made in France or the UK. There is also a quirky little museum dedicated to early 20th-century powder boxes.

🔲 E6 ✉ Via de' Tornabuoni 6 ☎ 055 286 925 🚌 6, 11, A

PAMPALONI

www.pampaloni.com

As well as ceramics, this high-quality gift shop aimed at the wedding-present market has a range of silverware and porcelain.

🔲 F6 ✉ Borgo Santi Apostoli 47r ☎ 055 289 094 🚌 B

PARENTI

Even those who say they don't like jewellery end up swooning over Parenti's eclectic mix of styles and shapes, ranging from art nouveau to sheer 1970s glitz.

🔲 E6 ✉ Via de' Tornabuoni 93r ☎ 055 214 438 🚌 6, 11, A

PARIONE

www.parione.it

This prestigious chain of stationers selling hand-decorated marbled paper, personalized stationery and accessories also has a collection of beautifully crafted music boxes and miniatures.

🔲 E6 ✉ Via Parione 10r ☎ 055 215 684 🚌 6, 11, A

PEGNA

www.pegna.it

This lovely old-fashioned shop, around since 1860, sells its delicious foods supermarket-style. Buy fine cheeses, olive oils, cakes, wines, salamis, chocolates and lots more.

🔲 F5 ✉ Via dello Studio 8 ☎ 055 282 701/2 🚌 A

PER BACCO

A welcome addition to the city, this *enoteca* conceals in its vaults more than 500 different Italian wines, with pride of place going to those produced locally. They prefer small firms for their attention to detail and eco-friendly production methods.

🔲 F6 ✉ Borgo SS. Apostoli 21/23r ☎ 055 292 646 🚌 B

PINEIDER
www.pineider.com
A chic and expensive stationery and bookbinding business that was founded in 1774. One of the characteristic papers covering diaries and address books is decorated with great artists' signatures.
F6 ✉ Piazza della Signoria 13–14r ☎ 055 284 655 🚌 A, B

PRADA–DONNA
www.prada.com
The world's most popular Italian fashion house of the moment. The headquarters are in Milan but there's a good range of women's clothes, shoes, bags and accessories in this branch.
E6 ✉ Via de' Tornabuoni 53r ☎ 055 267 471 🚌 6, 11, A

LA RINASCENTE
www.rinascente.it
This classy department store is where smart Florentines shop. It drips designer labels, although prices are good and there's the odd find to be made. There are also perfumery, lingerie and other departments for those who like to shop for everything under one roof.
F5 ✉ Piazza della Repubblica 1 ☎ 055 219 113 🚌 A

ROBERTO CAVALLI
www.robertocavalli.com
One of Tuscany's most renowned designers, known for his flamboyant styles using fur and wild prints. Relax at the café.
E6 ✉ Via de' Tornabuoni 83r ☎ 055 239 6226 🚌 6, 11, A

ROMANO
www.romanofirenze.com
For a huge variety of shoes, boots and sandals for both men and women, Romano has perhaps the most comprehensive selection. You'll see trendy young Florentines trying on kitten heels next to little old ladies looking at shoes that you didn't think were made any more. Not too pricey.
F5 ✉ Via Speziali 10r ☎ 055 216 535 🚌 A

SALVATORE FERRAGAMO
www.salvatoreferragamo.it
Designer shoes in the Palazzo Spini Feroni, which has a museum of

CLOTHES SHOPPING
The most exclusive designers are in the district of Via de' Tornabuoni and Via della Vigna Nuova. The area around Piazza della Repubblica and Via dei Calzaiuoli has a good range of major high-street clothes shops, such as MaxMara. In the streets east of Via dei Calzaiuoli there are many mid-range fashion boutiques. The areas around Santa Croce and San Lorenzo sell bargain fashions to the tourist market.

shoes (▷ 38). Considered to be the leading brand in Italian shoes and bags.
E6 ✉ Via de' Tornabuoni 4r–14r ☎ 055 292 123 🚌 6, 11, 22, 36, 37, A

SISLEY
Italian Sisleys have a much wider selection of fashion than their British counterparts, and the prices are up to 30 per cent lower, too. The Benetton subsidiary has a wide range of separates and accessories, as well as a number of the season's unmissable buys.
F5 ✉ Via Roma 11–13r ☎ 055 286 669 🚌 A

VALMAR
www.valmar-florence.com
A compact shop that sells trims and finishings for fashion and upholstery.
F6 ✉ Via Porta Rossa 53r ☎ 055 284 493 🚌 6, 11, A

VANDA NENCIONI
Pretty gilded frames, as well as period and modern prints.
F6 ✉ Via della Condotta 25r ☎ 055 215 345 🚌 A

VINARIUS
www.vinarius.net
Sample a glass before you buy at this elegant *enoteca*; experts will help you make your selection. Also local extra virgin olive oil, balsamic vinegar and delicacies made with truffles and honey.
G6 ✉ Borgo Santa Croce 15r ☎ 055 200 1216 🚌 13, 23, B, C

Entertainment and Nightlife

CHIESA DE'SANTA MARIA DE RICCI

During the free concerts held at 9.15 most nights, you can sample the distinctive sound of Florentine organ music. A wonderfully evocative setting for music similar to that heard here in the 13th century. Check for days.

F5 ⊠ Via del Corso ☎ 055 289 367 🚌 14, A

HARRY'S BAR

www.harrysbarfirenze.it

This American bar, on the banks of the Arno, is one of the best places for cocktails. The international food is good.

D6 ⊠ Lungarno Vespucci 22r ☎ 055 239 6700 🚌 B, D

LOONEES

This central, friendly, studenty basement bar is popular with tourists and has occasional live music playing mainly British and American classic covers.

F6 ⊠ Via Porta Rossa 15 ☎ 055 212 249 🚌 6, 11, A

MAYDAY

Locals swarm around this stylish music bar where, into the early hours, you can enjoy wine, good beer or a cocktail while listening to live music.

F6 ⊠ Via Dante Alighieri 16r ☎ 055 238 1290 🕐 Closed Sun 🚌 14, 23, A

ODEON CINEHALL

www.cinehall.it

Housed in the art nouveau Palazzo Strozzino,

the cinema has retained original sculptures, tapestries and a stained-glass cupola. Probably the best place in the city for original sound films in English.

E6 ⊠ Piazza Strozzi ☎ 055 214 068 🕐 Times vary. Check for schedule 🚌 6, 22, A

RED GARTER

Established in 1962, this American-style bar attracts students and younger tourists, and remains one of the most popular in the city. There is live music most nights, with cocktails and beers, food and live sports TV, too.

G6 ⊠ Via de' Benci 33r ☎ 055 234 4904 🕐 Daily 5pm–2am 🚌 14, 23

SLOWLY CAFÈ

www.slowlycafe.com

Chill out to eclectic music at this loft-inspired space. The trendy crowd sips classic cocktails and

---

EVENING STROLL

Going out in Florence in the evening doesn't have to mean actually going anywhere. In summer a really enjoyable and popular way of spending time after dinner is to stroll through the streets of the historic section, stopping off for an ice cream or a drink at a bar. What's more is that you'll see plenty of groups of Italians of all ages and genders doing exactly the same thing.

---

aperitifs while nibbling on Tuscan snacks.

F6 ⊠ Via Porta Rossa 63r ☎ 055 264 5354 🕐 Daily 7pm–2am 🚌 6, 11, A

TEATRO VERDI

Culture has always played an important part in the life of Florence and the Teatro Verdi was founded in 1854. The theatre puts on drama, ballet and opera from January to April. The excellent Orchestra della Toscana play here between December and May.

G6 ⊠ Via Ghibellina 99 ☎ 055 212 320 🚌 14, 23, A, C

TWICE

www.twiceclub.com

Go early for a drink, food or jazz, or wait until late when the pace picks up. You may want what's playing in advance. It's always popular, so expect a large crowd.

G6 ⊠ Via Giuseppe Verdi 57r ☎ 055 247 356 🕐 Nightly, bar opens 9pm. Late night schedule varies, check website 🚌 14, 23, A, C

YAB

www.yab.it

One of Florence's most central clubs, this is often full of young visitors. Music and fashions here are up-to-date. The theatrical surroundings add to the overall atmosphere.

F6 ⊠ Via Sassetti 5r ☎ 055 215 160 🕐 Closed some evenings, call for details. Closed Jun–Sep 🚌 6, 22, A

ENTERTAINMENT AND NIGHTLIFE

THE SOUTH CENTRO

ENTERTAINMENT AND NIGHTLIFE
THE SOUTH CENTRO

Restaurants

PRICES

Prices are approximate, based on a 3-course meal for one person.

€€€	over €45
€€	€20–€45
€	under €20

ALLE MURATE (€€€)

www.allemurate.it

Sophisticated restaurant where traditional Tuscan cooking is given an innovative twist. Try *tagliatelle all'olio nuovo tonne fresco, e timo* (wide noodles with freshly pressed olive oil, tuna and thyme). The soft lighting and candles make for an intimate dining experience.

➕ G6 ✉ Via del Proconsolo 16r ☎ 055 240 618 ⏰ Closed Mon 🚌 A

ANTICO BARILE (€€)

www.anticobarile.com

An excellent little restaurant that serves good Tuscan and international cuisine in the heart of city, close to Piazza Repubblica and the Duomo. The elegantly rustic setting has some interesting features and a mezzanine floor. Helpful service and competitive prices.

➕ F6 ✉ Via dei Cerchi 40r ☎ 055 213 142 🚌 14, 23, A

BALDOVINO (€€)

www.baldovino.com

Bustling trattoria not far from Piazza Santa Croce. Especially good for those with children as they serve great pizza, from a wood-burning oven, and the ambience is relaxed and not intimidating. The wide-ranging menu is constantly changing.

➕ H6 ✉ Via San Giuseppe 22r ☎ 055 241 773 🚌 14, C

BELLE DONNE (€–€€)

An inexpensive option in an expensive part of town. It's small, modest and you can barely see inside because of the potted plants. The menu has some interestingly prepared vegetables. You will probably share a table with others.

➕ E5 ✉ Via delle Belle Donne 16r ☎ 055 238 2609 🚌 36, 37, A, B

BOCCADAMA (€€)

www.boccadama.com

Interesting food and good wine, plus views of the

Basilica Santa Croce make this lively historic *enoteca* that doubles as a restaurant, very popular. You can eat on the delightful terrace, and enjoy dishes cooked with top quality local ingredients.

➕ G6 ✉ Piazza Santa Croce 25–26r ☎ 055 243 640 ⏰ Closed Tue dinner 🚌 14, 23, C

LA BUSSOLA (€€)

www.labussolafirenze.it

La Bussola serves some of the best pizza in town cooked in a traditional wood-burning oven; also good seafood dishes. In a rustic setting with a relaxed friendly service where you can eat from the bar.

➕ F6 ✉ Via Porta Rossa 58r ☎ 055 293 376 🚌 6, 11, A

CAFFÈ AMERINI (€€)

The Amerini lies in the main fashionable shopping area, and makes for a good venue for taking a break during the day. Be warned though—it gets very popular in the early afternoon. Snacks and a variety of pastries packed with tasty fillings.

➕ E6 ✉ Via della Vigna Nuova 63r ☎ 055 284 941 ⏰ Closed Sun 🚌 6, A

CANTINETTA DEI VERRAZZANO (€€)

A wonderful wine bar-cum-shop selling breads baked on the premises and wines from the Castello di Verrazzano estates near Greve. Don't miss the *focaccia* (flat

loaf), baked in the wood-burning ovens.
🇫 F6 ✉ Via de' Tavolini 18–20r ☎ 055 268 590 🕐 Closed Sun 🚌 A

IL CIBREO (€€€)
This restaurant, one of the city's gastronomic shrines, offers no pasta, but an intriguing range of robust Florentine dishes.
🇫 H6 ✉ Via Andea del Verrocchio 8r ☎ 055 234 1100 🕐 Closed Sun, Mon, and Aug 🚌 A

COCO LEZZONE (€€€)
Popular with Florentines, with informal white-tile rooms. The short menu offers Tuscan classics.
🇫 E6 ✉ Via del Parioncino 26r ☎ 055 287 178 🕐 Closed Tue dinner and Sun 🚌 6, A, B

DA BENVENUTO (€)
www.trattoriadabenvenuto.it
There's lots of solid Tuscan food to choose from at this long-standing venue in the Santa Croce quarter.
🇫 G6 ✉ Via della Mosca 16r ☎ 055 214 833 🚌 23, B

LA DECIMA MUSA (€€)
www.ladecimamusa.it
The refined and intimate atmosphere is largely thanks to its diminutive size and wood-panel walls. La Decima's patron Daniele Bertucci oversees a traditional but refined Tuscan menu and a first-class wine cellar.
🇫 E6 ✉ Via del Parione 50r

☎ 055 294 122 🕐 Closed Sun 🚌 6, 11, 22, A

DEI FRESCOBALDI RISTORANTE & WINE BAR (€€)
www.deifrescobaldi.it
On the corner of Piazza Signoria, Frescobaldi offers traditional Tuscan cuisine, or the chance to eat tapas Italian-style in the adjacent wine bar, including fresh salads, cheeses and salamis. In the main restaurant choose from tasty pasta dishes or substantial grilled meats. Excellent wine list.
🇫 F6 ✉ Via de' Magazzini 2–4r ☎ 055 284 724 🕐 Closed Sun, Mon lunch 🚌 14, 23, A

EITO (€€–€€€)
www.eito.it
This corner of Japan in Florence is where beautifully presented,

---

BREAD

Almost all bread in Tuscany is made without salt. This takes some getting used to, but the blandness makes a good background to highly seasoned foods such as the Florentine salami Finocchiona, which is scented with fennel and garlic. And the bread's texture—firm, almost coarse, and very substantial—is wonderful. Strict laws govern what goes into Italian bread: It is free of chemical preservatives.

---

refined Japanese cooking successfully attempts to arouse new sensations. The delightful ambience of this small restaurant creates a pleasant, relaxing and intimate atmosphere.
🇫 G6 ✉ Via dei Neri 72r ☎ 055 210 940 🕐 Dinner 7–11.30; closed Mon 🚌 23, B, C

ENOTECA PINCHIORRI (€€€)
www.enotecapinchiorri.it
The city's most fashion-able and priciest eatery is somewhat serious. For wine connoisseurs it is a must, possessing one of Europe's very finest wine cellars. Reserve ahead.
🇫 G6 ✉ Via Ghibellina 87 ☎ 055 242 777/757 🕐 Closed Sun–Wed lunch 🚌 14, A

GILLI (€€–€€€)
www.gilli.it
A chic, opulent café on the corner of the Piazza della Repubblica; the pastries are renowned (but pricey). Sit outside and indulge in, say, a lavish ice-cream sundae.
🇫 F5 ✉ Via Roma 1r ☎ 055 213 896 🕐 Closed Tue 🚌 6, 22, A

GIUBBE ROSSE (€€–€€€)
www.giubberosse.it
Once the haunt of futurists and the Florentine *avanguardia* scene. The red-jacketed waiters and stylish interiors hint at this illustrious past. Drink

coffee and watch the world go by on the elegant piazza.

🝰 F5 ✉ Piazza della Repubblica 13–14r ☎ 055 212 280 🚌 6, 22, A

GUSTO LEO (€–€€)

www.gustoleo.com

A good pitstop for lunch at the heart of the city, which attracts many young Italians to its excellent salads, pizza and soup.

🝰 G6 ✉ Via del Pronconsolo 8–10r ☎ 055 285 217 🚌 14, 23, A

HOSTARIA BIBENDUM (€€€)

www.hbf.royaldemeure.com

In the Hotel Helvetia & Bristol (▷ 112), this restaurant and cocktail bar exudes exclusivity. Expect gilt, chandeliers, draperies and a formal atmosphere. Safe but expertly prepared menu.

🝰 E5 ✉ Via dei Pescioni 8r ☎ 055 266 5620 🚌 6, 11, 22, A

INCANTO (€€€)

The lavish interiors of this renovated grand hotel restaurant have a striking contemporary feel. A well-balanced menu paying close attention to Tuscan tastes and fabulous desserts.

🝰 D5 ✉ Grand Hotel, Piazza Ognissanti 1 ☎ 055 2716 3767 🚌 A, B

KOME (€€)

www.komefirenze.it

A trendy sushi and BBQ restaurant in a historic palazzo between
walls under a gol
ceiling. Decorate
cool greens, high
stand alongside
winding counter.
from the kitchen
choose from the
tempting sushi train.

🝰 G6 ✉ Via de Benci 41r ☎ 055 200 8009 🛇 Closed Sun 🚌 14, 23

IL LATINI (€€)

www.illatini.com

Boisterous restaurant offering Tuscan classics such as *pappardelle con la lepre* (wide strips of pasta with hare sauce). Other interesting dishes include wild boar *dolce-forte* (wild boar stewed in honey, dried fuit and pine-nut sauce). Seating is at communal tables.

🝰 E5 ✉ Via dei Palchetti 6r ☎ 055 210 916 🛇 Closed Mon 🚌 A, B

PIZZA AT ITS BEST

As in every Italian town, pizzas are all over and many shops sell *pizza a taglio* (cut pizza). A good option for a quick snack is a slice. In addition to the standard margherita pizza (tomato and mozzarella), you will find all kinds of other delicious toppings, such as courgette (zucchini) flowers and aubergine (eggplant). Go when they're busy and the turnover is high to avoid eating cold pizza that's been sitting around for a while.

---

from including wild boar, guinea fowl and rabbit. Sublime soups, exquisite vegetables and innovative pasta creations.

🝰 E6 ✉ Via delle Terme 51r ☎ 055 287 643 🛇 Dinner only; closed Sun 🚌 6, 11, A, B

ORVM (€€€)

Dine in style in an elegant art deco setting at the Westin Excelsior Hotel, with views of the River Arno. Here you will find contemporary Mediterranean cuisine and Tuscan influences that promote healthy cooking using the finest seasonal ingredients.

🝰 D5 ✉ Piazza Ognissanti 3 ☎ 055 27161 🚌 36, 37, A, B, D

OSTERIA DE' BENCI (€)

A genuine Florentine *osteria*. Start with *crostini* (Tuscan *bruschetta*— toasted bread served with spreads, cheeses and cold meats) then choose from the day's menu that often includes spaghetti in red wine and/or a delicious vegetable soup. The meat is particularly good.

🝰 G6 ✉ Via de' Benci 13r ☎ 055 216 887 🛇 Closed Aug 🚌 14, 23, 71

PALLOTTIN
www.tratt
In bus
10

...O (€€)

...apallottino.com
...ness for nearly
...years, this traditional
...attoria near Santa Croce
has small dining rooms,
wooden tables and candles. It has a frequently
changing menu using
what's in season. Expect
excellent pasta dishes.
+ G6 ⊠ Via Isola delle
Stinche 1r ☎ 055 289 573
🕙 Closed Mon, Aug 🚌 14,
23, B

PASZKOWSKI (€€–€€€)

www.paszkowski.it
On the grandiose Piazza
della Repubblica, this is a
lovely, if expensive, old-
world café and tearoom
where a piano bar adds a
note of refinement to an
already delightful interior.
+ F5 ⊠ Piazza della
Repubblica 6r ☎ 055 213
896 🚌 6, 22, A

PERCHÉ NO! (€)

www.percheno.firenze.it
'Why not!' has to be a
good name for an ice-
cream place. Founded
in 1939, this shop still
produces plenty of new
tastes to get excited
about. It is renowned for
its *semifreddi*, which
come in creamy tastes
such as hazelnut mousse
and *zuppa inglese* (trifle).
+ F6 ⊠ Via dei Tavolini 19r
☎ 055 239 8969 🚌 6, A

PROCACCI (€–€€)

www.antinori.it
A delightful bar that is
something of a legend
because of its *panini
tartufati*, sandwiches
made with a white truffle
puree. Just the thing to
accompany a glass of
Tuscan wine.
+ E5 ⊠ Via de' Tornabuoni
64r ☎ 055 211 656 🚌 6,
11, A

RIVOIRE (€€–€€€)

www.rivoire.it
This café is a Florentine
institution. At Rivoire,
which opened in the
1870s, you pay for the
view, but it's worth it.
Looking out toward the
Palazzo Vecchio, this is
the ideal place to relax
after a hectic visit to
the Uffizi.
+ F6 ⊠ Piazza della
Signoria 5r ☎ 055 214 412
🕙 Closed Mon, 2 weeks in
Jan 🚌 A, B

TRATTORIA 13 GOBBI (€€)

www.casatrattoria.com
If you want character and
romantic ambience,
Gobbi oozes both with its
candlelight and warm

STAND OR SIT

You will almost always pay
a premium to sit down and
to enjoy the privilege of
waiter service at coffee
shops, cafés and gelateria
that often double up as all-
round bars to be enjoyed
during the day. If you stand,
which is less expensive, you
are generally not expected to
linger too long after finishing
your refreshment.

atmosphere. The
traditional Florentine and
Tuscan menu has been
given a lighter touch and
desserts are to die for.
+ D5 ⊠ Via del Porcellana
9r ☎ 055 284 015 🚌 B, D

TRATTORIA MARIONE (€)

www.casatrattoria.com
Good home cooking
based on local ingredients. Well-prepared dishes include *ribollito* (boiled
beef), soups and tripe.
+ E5 ⊠ Via della Spada 27r
☎ 055 214 756 🚌 36, 37, A

TRATTORIA PONTE VECCHIO (€€–€€€)

www.trattoriapontevecchio.com
A stone's throw from
the Ponte Vecchio, this
trattoria is inevitably popular with visitors and you
cannot fault the Tuscan
cuisine. One of the house
specials is tagliatelle with
porcini mushrooms.
+ F6 ⊠ Lungarno
Archibusieri 8r ☎ 055 292
289 🚌 B

VIVOLI (€)

www.vivoli.it
Vivoli is legendary; the
family have been making
ice cream since the
1930s. If you don't mind
the wait, the rewards are
delicious. Lots of choices,
including an extra creamy
mousse di amaretto.
All served in *coppette*
(different-size cups);
Vivoli is a no-cone zone.
+ G6 ⊠ Via Isola delle
Stinche 7r ☎ 055 292 334
🕙 Closed Mon 🚌 14, 23, A

The North Centro

A district abundant with fine churches, the epitome of which is the magnificent Duomo.

Palazzo
Pandolfini
Palazzo
Medici
Museo
Botanico
CAVOUR
Piazza
Isidoro
del Lungo
VIALE GIACOMO MATTEOTTI
San
Marco
Giardino
dei Semplici
Giardino
della
Gherardesca
Palazzo
Capponi
Piazzale
Donatello
Università
Gen M
Fanti
Piazza
San Marco
Santissima
Annunziata
Cimitero
degli Inglesi
Galleria
dell'Accademia
Museo di
Leonardo
da Vinci
Piazza di SS
Annunziata
Ferdinando I
Museo
Archeologico
Palazzo
Panciatichi-Ximenes
Ospedale
d Innocenti
Piazza
Brunelleschi
Ospedale
S Maria Nuova
Santa Maria
Maddalena
dei Pazzi
Piazza
Massimo
D'Azeglio
VIALE ANTONIO GRAMSCI
Teatro d
Pergola
Piazza di
Santa Maria
Nuova
Crocifisso
del Perugino
Museo Storico
Topografico
(Firenze com'era)
Sinagoga
Museo Nazionale
di Antropologia
e Etnologia
Volta di
S Piero
Piazza
G Salvemini
Pietrapiana
Borgo degli Albizi
V G Leopardi

G   H   J

Battistero

Perhaps the most loved of all Florence's edifices is the beautiful octagonal Baptistery referred to by Dante as his 'bel San Giovanni', and dedicated to St. John the Baptist, the city's patron saint.

Roman origins The Baptistery is one of the oldest buildings in the city: Remains of a Roman palace lie under it, and the dates given for the present construction vary between the fifth and the seventh centuries AD. For many centuries it was the place where Florentines were baptized and it is clear where the font stood until its removal in 1576.

Rich ornament The entire outer surface is covered with a beautiful design of white and green marble, added between the 11th and 13th centuries. Inside, the ceiling is encrusted with stunning mosaics: Above the altar, designs show the Virgin and St. John the Baptist; the main design depicts the *Last Judgement*, with the sinful being devoured by diabolical creatures, while the virtuous ascend to heaven. Do not miss the tessellated floor, almost Islamic in its intricate geometry.

Bronze doors The Baptistery is renowned, above all, for its bronze doors: the south doors, by Pisano (1336), and Ghiberti's north and east doors (1403–24 and 1425–52). The east doors, referred to by Michelangelo as the 'Gates of Paradise', are divided into 10 panels depicting Old Testament scenes. In 1990 copies of these doors replaced the originals, which are on view in the Museo dell'Opera del Duomo (▷ 62).

THE BASICS

www.operaduomo.firenze.it
➕ F5
✉ Piazza San Giovanni
☎ 055 230 2885
🕐 Mon–Sat 12.15–7 (first Sat of month 8.30–2), Sun, hols 8.30–2; last admission 30 min before closing
🚌 1, 14, 23, A
♿ Good
🎫 Moderate

HIGHLIGHTS

● 13th-century mosaics of the *Last Judgement*
● Ghiberti's east doors
● Pisano's south doors
● Zodiac pavement
● Romanesque marble exterior

Campanile

The superb bell tower affords fantastic views of the city—the climb is worth the effort

THE BASICS

➕ F5
✉ Piazza del Duomo
☎ 055 230 2885
🕐 Daily 8.30–7.30 (last admission 40 min before closing)
🚌 1, 14, 23, A
♿ Non-existent; no elevator
💰 Expensive

HIGHLIGHTS

● Views from the top
● Reliefs by Pisano and della Robbia

Tall and beautifully proportioned, the bell tower of the Duomo is one of the loveliest in Italy and adds a calm and graceful note to the otherwise busy cathedral complex.

Multiple effort The Campanile, or bell tower, of the Duomo rises to 85m (279ft). It was begun in 1334 and completed in 1359. Giotto was involved in its design, but by the time of his death in 1337 only the base had been completed. Andrea Pisano completed the second floor and the tower was finished by Francesco Talenti.

Relief sculpture The outer surface is decorated in the same polychrome marble as the Duomo: white marble from Carrara, green marble from Prato and pink marble from the Maremma. Around the bottom are two sets of relief sculptures: The lower tier is in hexagonal panels, the upper tier in diamonds. What you see are in fact copies; the originals have been moved to the Museo dell'Opera del Duomo (▶ 62) to prevent further atmospheric damage. The reliefs in the hexagonal panels, which were executed by Pisano (although some are believed to have been designed by Giotto), show the Creation of Man, the Arts and the Industries. On the north face are the five Liberal Arts (grammar, philosophy, music, arithmetic and astrology), executed by Luca della Robbia. The upper tier of reliefs, also the work of Pisano, illustrates the Seven Planets, the Seven Virtues and the Liberal Arts; the Seven Sacraments are attributed to Alberto Arnoldi.

Maddona and Child *by Michaelangelo (left); the Medici Chapels (right)*

Cappelle Medicee

Of all the places in Florence associated with Michelangelo, the Medici Chapels, the mausoleum of the Medici family, are the most intriguing: with tomb sculptures, *Madonna and Child*, and sketches.

Burial places The mausoleum of the Medici family is in three distinct parts of the church of San Lorenzo (▷ 64): the crypt, the Cappella dei Principi and the Sagrestia Nuova. The crypt was where the bodies of minor members of the dynasty were unceremoniously dumped. Tidied up in the 19th century, it now houses tomb slabs. In the Cappella dei Principi is a huge dome by Bernado Buontalenti, begun in 1604 and not completed until the 20th century. The inner surface is decorated in a heavy, grandiose way that speaks of political tyranny: The Medici coat of arms is rarely out of view. The tombs of six Medici Grand Dukes are in the chapel beneath the dome.

New Sacristy Right of the altar, the Sagrestia Nuova, built by Michelangelo between 1520 and 1534, is a reminder that the Medici were enlightened patrons. Michelangelo sculpted figures representing *Night and Day*, and *Dawn and Dusk* to adorn the tombs of Lorenzo, Duke of Urbino (1492–1519), and Giuliano, Duke of Nemours (1479–1516). The figure of *Night*, with moon, owl and mask, is one of his finest works. The *Madonna and Child* (1521) is by Michelangelo as well. In a room left of the altar are some superb charcoal drawings found in 1975 and attributed to Michelangelo.

THE BASICS

www.firenzemusei.it/medicee

⊞ F5

✉ Piazza Madonna degli Aldobrandini 6

☎ 055 238 8602

⊙ Daily 8.15–5 (last admission 30 min before closing); closed 1st, 3rd, 5th Mon, 2nd, 4th Sun of month and 1 Jan, 1 May, 25 Dec

🚍 1, 11, 17, A

♿ Poor; ask for assistance

💵 Expensive

❓ English audio guides (moderate)

HIGHLIGHTS

● Michelangelo's *Night*
● The figure of Lorenzo, Duke of Urbino
● Michelangelo's *Madonna and Child*
● Sketches attributed to Michelangelo
● Charcoal drawings by Michelangelo

Duomo

HIGHLIGHTS

● Brunelleschi's dome
● Santa Reparata remains
● Uccello's mural to a 14th-century Captain-General

TIP

● You will not be allowed into the Duomo wearing a sleeveless top or skimpy shorts.

The famous dome of this cathedral dominates the Florence skyline, with its eight white ribs on a background of terracotta tiles. From close up, the size of the building is overwhelming.

Long-term build The cathedral of Santa Maria del Fiori, the Florence Duomo, is a vast Gothic structure built on the site of the 7th-century church of Santa Reparata, whose remains can be seen in the crypt. It was built at the end of the 13th century, although the colossal dome, which dominates the exterior, was not added until the 15th century, and the facade was not finished until the 19th century. The exterior is a decorative riot of pink, white and green marble; the interior is stark and plain. The clock above the entrance on the west wall inside was designed in 1443 by

Clockwise from left: Crowds gather beneath the Duomo; the cupola is crowned by a lantern; intricate detail enhances the cathedral; Dante and his Worlds; detail inside the cathedral; The Last Judgement; viewed from a height, the cupola is the glory of the Duomo

Paolo Uccello in line with the *ora italica*, according to which the 24th hour of the day ends at sunset.

Roman influences Built by Filippo Brunelleschi, who won the competition for its commission in 1418, the dome is egg-shape and was made without scaffolding. Its herringbone brickwork was copied from the Pantheon in Rome. The best way to see the dome is to climb its 463 steps. The route takes you through the interior, where you can see Vasari's much-reviled frescoes of the *Last Judgement* (1572–79), and toward the lantern, from which the views are fantastic.

Explosion At Easter the *Scoppio del Carro*, a Mass-cum-theatrical pageant, ends with a mechanical dove being launched from the altar along a wire to the entrance, igniting a cart of fireworks.

THE BASICS

www.operaduomo.firenze.it

⊞ F5

✉ Piazza del Duomo

☎ 055 230 2885

🕐 Cathedral Mon–Wed 10–5, Thu 10–3.30, Sat 10–4.45 (1st Sat of month 10–3.30), Sun, hols 1.30–4.45. Dome (access from north side of cathedral at Porta della Mandoria) Mon–Fri 8.30–7, Sat 8.30–5.40 (last admission 40 min before closing)

🚌 1, 14, 23, A

♿ Good (access via Porta di Canonica, south side)

💷 Free; dome expensive; crypt moderate

Galleria dell'Accademia

HIGHLIGHTS

● Michelangelo's *David*
● Michelangelo's *Prisoners*
● Giambologna's *Rape of the Sabine Women*
● Buonaguida's *Tree of Life*

TIP

● If you want to view *David*, arrive when the museum first opens, or late in the day, to avoid the long lines.

Michelangelo's *David*, exhibited in the Accademia, has a powerful impact: the intensity of his gaze, that assured posture, those huge hands, the anatomical precision of the veins and the muscles.

Art School The Accademia was founded in 1784 to teach techniques of painting, drawing and sculpture. Since 1873 it has housed the world's single most important collection of sculptures by Michelangelo. There are also sculptures by other artists, as well as many paintings, mostly from the Renaissance period.

Masterpiece The main attraction is the *David* by Michelangelo, sculpted in 1504 and exhibited outside the Palazzo Vecchio until 1873, when it was transferred to the Accademia to protect it from

St. Francis Receiving the Stigmata, an exhibit in the Galleria dell'Academia (left);
The Tree of Life or Jesse's Tree by Pacino di Buonaguida is preserved in the gallery
(middle); the most famous and most visited or all statues in Florence, the magnificent
sculpture of David by Michelangelo (right)

environmental damage. It captures the moment
at which the young David contemplates defying
the giant Goliath. After controversial restoration
techniques, David was unveiled in June 2004.

Freedom from stone The *Prisoners* (1505) were
made for the tomb of Pope Julius II. The title refers
to Michelangelo's belief that when he sculpted a
statue, he was freeing the figure from the marble,
and the style, particularly preferred by Michelangelo,
was called the *non finito* (unfinished). After his
death, the *Prisoners* were moved to the Grotta
Grande in the Boboli Gardens (▷ 82), where the
originals were replaced with casts in 1908. Also
seek out the original plaster model for *The Rape
of the Sabine Women* (1583), Giambologna's last
work; the marble version is in the Loggia dei Lanzi
in Piazza della Signoria (▷ 32).

THE BASICS

www.polomuseale.firenze.it
✚ G4
✉ Via Ricasoli 58–60
☎ 055 238 8609
🕐 Tue–Sun 8.15–6.50;
closed 1 May (last
admission 30 min before
closing)
🚌 1, 17, C
♿ Good
✋ Expensive

Museo dell'Opera del Duomo

Detail of a dancing choir by Lucca della Robbia (left); a fresco in the museum (right)

THE BASICS

www.operaduomo.firenze.it

+ G5

✉ Piazza del Duomo 9

☎ 055 230 2885

🕐 Daily 9–7.30 (Sun until 1.45)

🚌 1, 14, 23, A

& Good

💶 Expensive

HIGHLIGHTS

● Singing galleries
● Original panels from the Campanile
● Michelangelo's *Pietà*
● Original panels from the 'Gates of Paradise'
● Donatello's *Maddalena*

There is something very pleasing about the idea of visiting the Cathedral Workshop, the maintenance section of the huge artistic undertaking that the cathedral complex represents.

Refuge from pollution This workshop-museum was founded when the Duomo was built, to maintain the art of the cathedral. Its location was chosen in the 15th century, and it was in its court-yard that Michelangelo sculpted his *David*. Since 1891 it has housed works from the cathedral complex, leaving the Duomo rather empty of art. It is also a refuge for outdoor sculptures.

Michelangelo's *Pietà* On the first level you can see eight of the original ten bronze panels from the east door of the Bapistery by Lorenzo Ghiberti. On the main landing is the *Pietà* (begun c1550) by Michelangelo. It is said he intended it for his own tomb; the hooded figure of Nicodemus is often interpreted as a self-portrait. The damage to Christ's left leg and arm is believed to have been inflicted by Michelangelo in frustration at his failing skills.

Artists compared The main room on the first floor contains two *cantorie* (singing galleries) that once stood in the Duomo: one by Luca della Robbia (1431–38), the other by Donatello (1433–39). In the room on the left are panels by Pisano from the Campanile (▷ 56); the next room has the construction materials and instruments used for Brunelleschi's dome, such as pulleys and brick moulds.

Opulence in the Palazzo Medici-Riccardi (left); fresco by Luca Giordano (right)

Palazzo Medici-Riccardi

The Medici family ruled with a mixture of tyranny and humanity, and this is reflected in the imposing facade of their huge headquarters, with its fearsome lattice of window bars.

Medici origins The Palazzo Medici-Riccardi, now mostly government offices, was the seat of the Medici family from its completion in 1444 until 1540, when Cosimo I moved the Medici residence to the Palazzo Vecchio and this palace was bought by the Riccardi family.

Setting a trend The palace, designed by Michelozzo, was widely imitated in Florence, for example in the Palazzo Strozzi and the Palazzo Pitti (▷ 84–85). It is characterized by huge slabs of stone, rusticated to give a roughly hewn rural appearance. The courtyard is in a lighter style, with a graceful colonnade and black and white *sgraffito* decoration of medallions, based on the designs of Roman intaglios collected by the Medici and displayed in the Museo degli Argenti (▷ 85).

A regal scene Steps right of the entrance lead to the Cappella dei Magi. This tiny chapel has the dazzling fresco cycle depicting the *Journey of the Magi* (1459–63) that Piero de' Medici commissioned from Gozzoli in memory of the Compagnia dei Magi, a religious organization to which the Medici belonged. Portraits of the Medici are believed to have been incorporated into the cast of characters, while the procession recalls the pageantry of the Compagnia dei Magi.

THE BASICS

www.palazzo-medici.it
🔲 F5
✉ Via Cavour 3
☎ 055 276 0340
🕐 Thu–Tue 9–7
🚌 1, 6, 7, 17
♿ Entrance on Via Cavour; Cappella poor
💶 Expensive
❓ Entrance to chapel limited to eight visitors every seven minutes

HIGHLIGHTS

● Gozzoli's fresco cycle of the *Journey of the Magi* (1459–63)
● Compagnia dei Magi (Chapel of the Magi) with enchanting animals

San Lorenzo

The Basilica di San Lorenzo (left); the serene cloisters of San Lorenzo (right)

THE BASICS

* F5
* Piazza San Lorenzo
* 055 214 042
* Nov–Feb Mon–Sat 10–5.30; Mar–Oct 1.30–5.30
* 1, 11, 6, 17, A
* Poor
* Moderate

HIGHLIGHTS

* Biblioteca Laurenziana (begun 1524)
* Staircase by Michelangelo
* Bronzino's *Martyrdom of St. Lawrence*
* Pulpits by Donatello
* Brunelleschi's Sagrestia Vecchia

San Lorenzo is the parish church and burial place of the Medici and is filled with art commissioned by them. As with the Cappelle Medicee, it is a monument to the family's artistic patronage.

A sacred site San Lorenzo was rebuilt by Filippo Brunelleschi 1425–46, on the site of one of the city's oldest churches (consecrated in AD393). Its rough-hewn ochre exterior was to have been covered with a facade by Michelangelo. This was never added, but a model is in Casa Buonarroti (▷ 37). The most bizarre piece of art here is the statue of Anna Maria Luisa (d1743), the last of the Medici dynasty, found—like a displaced Limoges porcelain figure—outside of the church. The church, with its *pietra serena* (grey sandstone) columns, is cool and airy. The bronze pulpits (c1460) depicting the Resurrection and scenes from the life of Christ are Donatello's last work. Bronzino's fresco (facing the altar, left) of the *Martyrdom of St. Lawrence* (1569) is an absorbing Mannerist study of the human body in various contortions. Inside Sagrestia Vecchia (Old Sacristy, 1421) are eight *tondi* (circular reliefs) by Donatello depicting the evangelists and scenes from the life of St. John.

Biblioteca Laurenziana The Laurentian Library (tel 055 210 760, www.bml.firenze.sbn.it; Mon–Thu 8–5.30, Fri 8–2) houses the Medici's collection of manuscripts (not on display). This extraordinary example of Mannerist architecture by Michelangelo is left of the church, up a curvaceous *pietra serena* staircase via the cloisters.

The Annunication by
Fra Angelico (left);
the ornate exterior of
San Marco (right)

San Marco

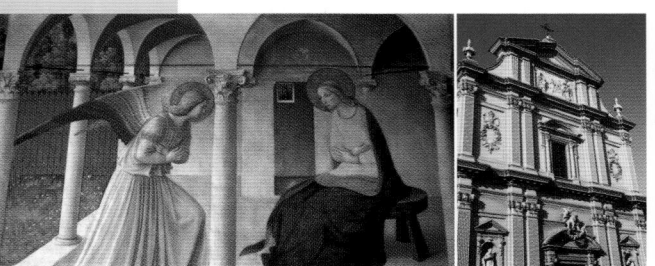

Dominated by the lovely paintings of Fra Angelico, the soothing convent of San Marco has an aura of monastic calm that is conducive to appreciating the religious themes depicted.

Medici motives San Marco was founded in the 13th century by Silvestrine monks. In 1437 Cosimo il Vecchio invited the Dominican monks of Fiesole to move into the convent and had it rebuilt by Michelozzo, a gesture motivated by his guilt for his wealth from banking and that the Dominicans were useful allies. Ironically, Savonarola, who denounced the decadence of the Medici at the end of the 15th century, came to prominence as the Dominican prior of San Marco.

A feast for the eyes The Chiostro di Sant' Antonino, the cloister through which you enter, is decorated with faded frescoes by Fra Angelico and other Florentine artists. In the Ospizio dei Pellegrini, where pilgrims were cared for, there is a superb collection of freestanding paintings by Fra Angelico and his followers. At the top of the stair-case on the way to the dormitory is Fra Angelico's *Annunciation* (1440), an image of great tender-ness and grace. Each of the 44 monks' cells is adorned with a small fresco by Fra Angelico or one of his assistants. The themes include the *Entombment* (cell 2) and the *Mocking of Christ* (cell 7). Savonarola's rooms house an exhibition about him. Cells 38 and 39 were reserved for Cosimo il Vecchio, who periodically spent time in the monastery.

THE BASICS

www.polomuseale.firenze.it
➕ G4
✉ Piazza San Marco 3
☎ 055 238 8608
🕐 Church: daily 7–12, 4–8. Museum: Mon–Fri 8.30–1.50, Sat, Sun 8.15–4.50; closed 1st, 3rd, 5th Sun, 2nd, 4th Mon of month
🚌 1, 6, 7, 10, 11, 17, 20, 25, 31, 32, 33, C
♿ Acceptable
💲 Moderate

HIGHLIGHTS

● Fra Angelico's cell paintings
● Fra Angelico's *Annunciation*
● Savonarola's cells
● Cosimo il Vecchio's cells

Santa Maria Novella

Santa Maria Novella's intricate facade makes an excellent perch for passing visitors

HIGHLIGHTS

● Marble facade
● Masaccio's *Trinità*
● Cappellone degli Spagnoli
● Tornabuoni Chapel
● Brunelleschi's wooden crucifix (1420) in Cappella Gondi

The decorative marble facade of Tuscany's most important Gothic church incorporates billowing sails (emblem of Alberti's patron, Rucellai) and ostrich feathers (emblem of the Medici).

Dominican origins The church of Santa Maria Novella was built between 1279 and 1357 by Dominican monks. The lower part of the marble facade, Romanesque in style, is believed to be by Fra Jacopo Talenti; the upper part was completed between 1456 and 1470 by Leon Battista Alberti.

Deceptive interior Inside, the church is vast and looks even longer than it is, thanks to the clever spacing of the columns. As you face the altar, on the left-hand side is a fresco of the *Trinità* (c1428) by Masaccio, one of the earliest paintings to demonstrate mastery of perspective. Many of the chapels are named after the church's wealthy patrons. The Strozzi Chapel (left transept) is dedicated to St. Thomas Aquinas and decorated with frescoes (1351–57) by Nardo di Cione depicting *Heaven and Hell*: Dante himself is represented in the *Last Judgement* just behind the altar. The Tornabuoni Chapel contains Ghirlandaio's fresco cycle of the life of St. John the Baptist (1485) in contemporary costume. The Cappellone degli Spagnoli ('Spanish Chapel'), was used by the courtiers of Eleanor of Toledo, wife of Cosimo I. In the frescoes *Triumph of the Doctrine* (c1365) by Andrea da Firenze, the dogs of God (a pun on the word Dominican—*domini canes*) are sent to round up lost sheep into the fold of the church.

A scene from *Life of Saint Benizzi (left)* in *Santissima Annunziata* church *(right)*

Santissima Annunziata

The intimacy and delicate architecture of the Piazza della SS. Annunziata contrast with the grandeur of much of Florence. The roundels of babies on the Ospedale degli Innocenti are quite enchanting.

Old New Year The Feast of the Annunciation on 25 March used to be New Year in the old Florentine calendar, and for that reason the church and the square have always played a special role in the life of the city. Every year, on 25 March, a fair is still held in the square and special biscuits called *brigidini* are sold.

Wedding flowers The church of Santissima Annunziata was built by Michelozzo in 1444–81 on the site of a Servite oratory. Entry is through an atrium known as the Chiostrino dei Voti (1447), which has the air of a rickety greenhouse though the frescoes inside are superb. They include Rosso Fiorentino's *Assumption*, Pontormo's *Visitation* and Andrea del Sarto's *Birth of the Virgin*. The church is dedicated to the Virgin Mary due to the legend that a painting of the Virgin was started by a monk in 1252 and finished by an angel. Newlyweds have traditionally brought their wedding bouquet to the church to ensure a happy marriage.

Early orphanage The Spedale degli Innocenti, on the east side of the piazza, was the first orphanage in Europe. A small museum includes works by major artists from the 14th to the 18th centuries. Designed by Brunelleschi in 1419, it has enamel terracotta roundels by della Robbia (1498).

THE BASICS

⊞ G4
✉ Piazza della SS. Annunziata
☎ 055 266 181. Spedale degli Innocenti 055 203 7308
🕐 Daily 7.30–12.30, 4–6.30; closed during services. Spedale daily 8.30–7 (Sun until 2)
🚌 6, 31, 32, C
♿ Good
💶 Free to church; moderate to Spedale

HIGHLIGHTS

● Andrea della Robbia's roundels
● Facade of the Spedale degli Innocenti
● Rosso Fiorentino's *Assumption*
● Pontormo's *Visitation*
● Andrea del Sarto's *Birth of the Virgin*

More to See

GIARDINO DEI SEMPLICI

This oasis of neat greenery, the botanical garden of Florence University, is on the site of a garden laid out in 1545–46 for Cosimo I, who wanted to keep up with the Pisans and Genoans. It is named after the medicinal plants (*semplici*) grown here. There are also greenhouses with tropical palms, orchids and citrus fruits.

�`+` G4 ✉ Via Micheli 3 ☎ 055 275 7402 🕐 Mon–Tue, Thu–Fri 9–1, Sat 9–5 🚌 1, 7, 25 ♿ Good 👆 Inexpensive

MERCATO CENTRALE

The largest of Florence's produce markets held in the magnificent cast-iron structure of the Mercato Centrale, built in 1874, with an extra floor added in 1980.

�`+` F4 ✉ Via dell'Ariento 🕐 Jul–Aug Mon–Sat 7–2; Sep–Jun Mon–Fri 7–2, Sat 7–5 🚌 12, 25, 33 ♿ Good (but crowded)

MERCATO SAN LORENZO

Fun, touristy and centrally located in the shadow of the church of San Lorenzo. Lots of stalls sell leather goods, many of which are genuinely good value, but go armed with a healthy scepticism.

�`+` F5 ✉ Piazza San Lorenzo 🕐 Daily 9–7.30 🚌 1, 6, 11, 17 ♿ Good

MUSEO ARCHEOLOGICO

One of the best places to see Etruscan art. There are also Roman, Greek and Egyptian exhibits. Notable is the rare collection from Kafiri, north Pakistan.

�`+` H4 ✉ Palazzo della Crocetta, Via della Colonna 36 ☎ 055 23575 🕐 Mon 2–7, Tue, Thu 8.30–7, Wed, Fri–Sun 8.30–2 🚌 6, 31, 32, C ♿ Good 👆 Moderate

MUSEO BOTANICO

www.msn.unifi.it

A collection of Florence University, the museum, founded in 1842, houses 4 million specimens—the largest and most important collection of its kind in Italy. Be sure to see the Andrea Cesalpino Herbarium and the wax models of plants.

�`+` G3 ✉ Via La Pira 4 ☎ 055 275 7462 🕐 By appointment only; call first 🚌 1, 7, 25 ♿ Good 👆 Free

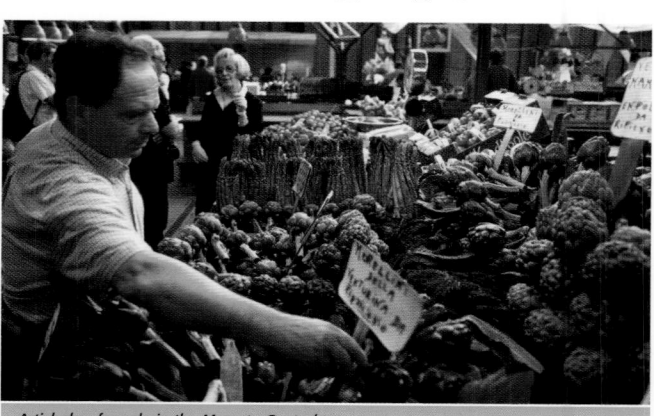
Artichokes for sale in the Mercato Centrale

MUSEO DI LEONARDO DA VINCI

www.mostredileonardo.com

This exhibition complex is dedicated to the 'genius of Leonardo' and displays some 40 models of his inventions. Categories cover machines connected to the elements of earth, fire, water and air, with a fifth section devoted to mechanical devices. Visitors can manoeuvre the machines, which have been reconstructed in wood, metal and textiles.

➕ G5 ✉ Via dei Servi 66–68 ☎ 055 282 966 🕔 Daily 10–7 🚍 14, 23, C ♿ Good 💷 Expensive

MUSEO NAZIONALE DI ANTROPOLOGIA E ETNOLOGIA

www.msn.unifi.it

Founded in 1869 (part of Florence University), this museum offers more than just art and history. The people of the areas of Africa that came under Italian colonial rule are represented.

➕ G5 ✉ Palazzo Nonfinito, Via del Proconsolo 12 ☎ 055 239 6449 🕔 Mon–Tue, Thu–Fri, Sun 9–1, Sat 9–5 🚍 14, 23, A ♿ Good 💷 Moderate

MUSEO STORICO TOPOGRAFICO (FIRENZE COM'ERA)

Paintings and maps showing how Florence was from the late 15th until the early 20th centuries. There's also 16th-century lunettes of the Medici villas, and the Pianta della Catena, an 1887 copy of a 1470 view of Florence.

➕ G5 ✉ Via dell'Oriuolo 24 ☎ 055 261 6545 🕔 Jun–end Sep Mon–Tue 9–2, Sat 9–7; Oct–end May Mon–Wed 9–2, Sat 9–7 🚍 14, 23, A ♿ Good 💷 Inexpensive

SANTA MARIA MADDALENA DEI PAZZI

Although the original church dates from the 13th century, most of the present building is a Renaissance rebuild designed by Guiliano da Sangallo at the end of the 15th century. The spectacular interior decoration, with its marble and *trompe l'oeil*, dates from the baroque. The highlight here is in the fresco of the 1490s by Perugino in the chapter house (reached via the crypt).

➕ H5 ✉ Borgo Pinti 58 🕔 Mon–Sat 9–12, 4.45–5.20, 6.15–6.50, Sun 9–10.45, 5–6.50 🚍 6, C ♿ Poor 💷 Inexpensive

Trompe l'oeil *in Santa Maria Maddalena dei Pazzi*

A large painted mummy case in the Museo Archeologico

North of the City

Taking in Florence's main market area and the most important churches and galleries in the northern part of the city.

DISTANCE: 3km (2 miles) **ALLOW:** Full morning

START

CAPPELLE MEDICEE (▷ 57)
🗺 F5 🚌 1, 11, 17, A

END

SANTISSIMA ANNUNZIATA (▷ 67)
🗺 G4 🚌 6, 31, 32, C

WALK

THE NORTH CENTRO

1 Start at the Cappelle Medicee (▷ 57), in Piazza Madonna degli Aldobrandini, the last resting place of many of the Medici family.

2 The church of San Lorenzo (▷ 64) itself (entered from Piazza San Lorenzo) is a masterpiece of Renaissance church design. Inside are works by Donatello.

3 Explore the market north of San Lorenzo; cut through the Mercato Centrale (▷ 68) and return to Piazza San Lorenzo. The Palazzo Medici-Riccardi (▷ 63) is on the north side.

4 Follow Via Cavour and take the second left into Via degli Arazzieri, follow into Via XXVII Aprile to reach the former convent of Sant' Apollonia, with a fresco of the *Last Supper* by Andrea del Castagno.

8 Across the square is the Ospedale degli Innocent. If time permits go inside to see the modest museum and the two Brunelleschi cloisters.

7 This is one of the city's most distinctive squares. The square's church, Santissima Annunziata (▷ 67), is known for its frescoes by Andrea del Santo and others.

6 The ex-convent on the north side of the square houses Museo di San Marco (▷ 65), devoted to the works of Fra Angelico. Continue eastward along Via Cesare Battisti to Piazza della Santissima Annunziata.

5 Walk east to Piazza San Marco, pausing to view Michelangelo's *David* in the Galleria dell'Accademia (▷ 60–61)

Shopping

ABACUS

www.abacusfirenze.it

The sign on the door says that this bookbindery aspires to 'sturdiness and beauty'. The hand-stitched spines and exquisitely lined covers make the volumes exceptional gifts. For such good quality, the prices are surprisingly low.

✚ F4 ✉ Via de'Ginori 28–30r ☎ 055 219 719 🚍 1, 6, 7, 10

ALICE'S MASKS ART STUDIO

www.alicemasks.com

Papier-mâché in all shapes and sizes are here: animals—mythical and real—as well as more theatrical and surreal characters. They are all hand painted and finished.

✚ E4 ✉ Via Faenza 72r ☎ 055 287 370 🚍 4, 12, 25, 33

ARTE CRETA

Admire artist Elisabetta di Costanzo painting her majolica fresh from the kiln in brilliant hues. Her delightful pieces make a refreshing souvenir.

✚ G6 ✉ Via del Proconsolo 63r ☎ 055 284 341 🚍 14, 23, A

BARTOLINI

www.dinobartolini.it

A Florentine institution; the junction where it stands is referred to as 'Bartolini corner'. It sells just about every item of kitchenware you could wish for, as well as fine china and porcelain. All the worldwide names are here but look out for the Italian ceramics such as Italian Arts and Solimene-Vietri ware.

✚ G5 ✉ Via dei Servi 30 ☎ 055 211 895 🚍 14, 23, C

BLUNAUTA

This Italian chain sells funky, natural fabric casual clothing that looks good on all generations.

✚ G5 ✉ Via del Proconsolo 69r ☎ 055 212 460 🚍 4, 23, A

BORGO

www.borgovino.com

This small, tempting and well-stocked wine shop focuses on smaller local winemakers. Cheryl, the American lady who runs the shop with her Italian husband, is a font of knowledge. Also *biscotti,* pasta and olive oil.

✚ E5 ✉ Borgo San Lorenzo 20r ☎ 055 215 103 🚍 1, 6, 7, 10, 11, 14

BOTTEGA ORAFA PENKO

www.penkofirenze.it

Master goldsmith Paolo

MARBLED PAPER

The skill of marbling paper was brought to Florence from Venice, where it had been learned from the East in the 12th century. Today's Florentine paper goods range greatly in price and quality, but even the inexpensive goods are attractive—and easily transported.

Penco makes jewellery to order using techniques that originate from the Renaissance period.

✚ F5 ✉ Via F Zannetti 14 ☎ 055 211 661 🚍 1, 6, 11, A

LA BOTTEGHINA DEL CERAMISTA

The vivid and lively patterns that are hand painted on these jugs, bowls and dishes will brighten any table.

✚ F4 ✉ Via Guelfa 5r ☎ 055 287 367 🚍 1, 6, 7, 10, 11, 17

CASA DEL VINO

www.casadelvino.it

This wine shop has occupied the same premises since it first opened in the second half of the 19th century. Today it has a very well-stocked cellar with nearly 1,000 wines from around the world. You are invited to sample wine by the glass and have a snack while making a decision.

✚ F4 ✉ Via dell'Ariento 16r ☎ 055 215 609 🚍 12, 25, 33

CORNICI CAMPANI

This artisan shop has been dedicated to making handcrafted frames for paintings since 1889. The founder, Gino Campani was a well-known collector and celebrated frame maker. Custom-made frames take about one week to complete.

✚ G5 ✉ Via dei Servi 22r ☎ 055 216 984 🚍 14, 23, C

ECHO

www.echofirenze.it

It's doubtful you'll have ever heard of any of the labels in this shop but you're sure to be bowled over by the clever designs. Go through the rails and check out the reasonable prices. A younger, funkier Echo is located next door.

G5 ✉ Via dell' Oriuolo 37–39r ☎ 055 238 1149 🚍 14, 23

ERMENI

www.erminiagostino.com

This bizarre fabric shop seems stuck in a time warp, but it's worth visiting for some good value linen. There are also some more lavish fabrics for upholstering and soft furnishings.

F5 ✉ Via Borgo San Lorenzo 3r ☎ 055 292 200 🚍 1, 6, 7, 10, 11, 14, 17, 23

FRATELLI ALINARI

www.alinari.com

For the kind of postcards you want to keep rather than send, Alinari's, established in 1852, has an awesome archive that includes some of the first photographs ever taken in Italy. You can order any print for a very reasonable price. It also sells beautiful coffee-table books.

E5 ✉ Largo Alinari 15 ☎ 055 23951 🚍 4, 12, 25

FRETTE

This world-famous Italian company produces refined superior fabrics for the home, always at the cutting edge of fashion; bedding, tableware and lots more.

G4 ✉ Via Cavour 2r ☎ 055 211 369 🚍 1, 6, 7, 10, 11, 17, 31, 32, A

HERMÈS

www.hermes.com

The biggest and best-equipped branch in Italy of the classically elegant Paris-based designer.

E5 ✉ Piazza Antinori 6r ☎ 055 238 1004 🚍 6, 11, 22, 36, 37, A

INTIMISSIMI

The simple cotton and silk lingerie and sleepwear is hard to beat in terms of quality and price. You can be assured a good service.

E5 ✉ Via de Cerretani 15r ☎ 055 239 9132 🚍 1, 14, 23, A

SHOE CITY

The Florentines are famed for making superb shoes. As a testament to the historical importance of the industry in the city's economy, one of the main streets in Florence is named after the shoemakers (Calzaiuoli). The range of shoes available is vast, from the pinnacle of international chic to the value-for-money styles for sale in the market of San Lorenzo. Showrooms at the leather 'factories' in the Santa Croce area are worth a visit.

LIBRERIA ANTIQUARIA GONNELLI

www.gonnelli.it

For more than a century collectors have been coming to this historic bookshop to uncover old and rare books, stamps and manuscripts.

G4 ✉ Via Ricasoli 14r ☎ 055 216 835 🚍 14, 23, C

LORETTA CAPONI

www.lorettacaponi.com

Feminine linens, nightclothes and lingerie for mother and daughter.

E5 ✉ Piazza Antinori 4r ☎ 055 213 668 🚍 6, 11, 22, 23, 36, 37, A

MAXMARA

www.maxmara.com

Classic elegance takes precedence over ostentation; clothes are of superb quality, beautifully tailored and at reasonable prices.

F5 ✉ Via dei Pecori 23r ☎ 055 287 761 🚍 6, A

ORNAMENTA

This little shop sells small amber rings and silver earrings along with more ethnic styles at reasonable prices.

G5 ✉ Via Proconsolo 65 ☎ 055 292 879 🚍 14, 23, A

OSTERIA DE L'ORTOLANO

www.osteriafirenze.com

A must for fans of Italian food, this excellent delicatessen and catering company has been in business since 1962. Pick up a complete meal to

take out or souvenirs to bring home such as biscuits, jams and sauces.
➕ G5 ✉ Via degli Alfani 91r ☎ 055 239 6466 🚌 1, 6, 7, 10, 11, 17

IL PAPIRO
www.ilpapirofierenze.it
These shops in central Florence sell excellent marbled paper goods in particularly pretty shades. These include little chests of drawers and tiny jewellery boxes. At four other locations in the city.
➕ G4 ✉ Via Cavour 59r ☎ 055 215 262 🚌 1, 6, 10, 11, 17

PASSAMANERIA TOSCANA FIRENZE
www.ptfsrl.com
This shop sells furnishing fabrics, brocades, tassels and other trimmings as well as cushions and footstools. The shades and textures are rich and sensuous, the whole experience bordering on the utterly abandoned.
➕ F5 ✉ Piazza San Lorenzo 12r ☎ 055 214 670 🚌 1, 6, 11, 17

LE PIETRE NELL'ARTE
www.scarpellimosaici.it
A really classy shop run by the Scarpelli family. They sell beautiful hard and semiprecious stone inlays, interior decorations and artistic objects including sculptures, tables, pictures, brooches and much more. The stones used included onyx, chalcedony, malachite and jasper.

➕ F5 ✉ Piazza Duomo 36r ☎ 055 212 587 🚌 1, 14, 23, A

RASPINI
www.raspini.com
A few steps from the Duomo, this fashion store is known for giving a platform to new young designers, and there is no shortage of prestigious labels on offer. There are branches at Via Roma 25r and Via Por Santa Maria 72r, and Raspini Vintage at Via Calimaruzza 17r.
➕ F5 ✉ Via Martelli 5–7r ☎ 055 239 8336 🚌 1, 6, 7, 11, 17, A

RICHARD GINORI
Florence's own porcelain designer who also does dinner services to order with your family crest, a picture of your home or

<table>
<tr><td colspan="1">

CHIANTI

Chianti gets its name from the region in which it is made. Sangiovese grapes are harvested in October, pressed and then the juice and skins of the grapes are fermented for about 15 days, after which the juice alone is given a second fermentation. In spring the wine is matured in wooden casks. *Chianti Classico* is usually regarded as the best of the seven types of Chianti. This is produced in the eponymous region north of Siena. Wines of the Chianti Classico Consortium bear the symbol of the Gallo Nero (black cockerel).
</td></tr>
</table>

whatever else you want.
➕ E5 ✉ Via Rondinelli 17r ☎ 055 210 041 🚌 6, 11, A

SBIGOLI TERRECOTTE
www.sbigoliterrecotte.it
Pots designed, painted and fired in Florence by the family owners. The designs come in majolica and tactile unglazed terracotta and at good prices.
➕ G5 ✉ Via Sant'Egidio 4r ☎ 055 247 9713 🚌 14, 23

SCRIPTORIUM
www.scriptoriumfirenze.com
This shop draws on two great Florentine crafts—leather working and papermaking—to create objects of beauty and refined taste. The plain paper books are notable, bound with soft leather in subdued natural shades.
➕ G5 ✉ Via dei Servi 5–7r ☎ 055 211 804 🚌 14, 23, C

TERRE DEI GIGLI
www.terredeigigli.it
The best virgin olive oil, Tuscan ragu, *crostino* and *cantuccini* biscuits are just a sample of the Tuscan fare crammed into this tiny deli, which is housed in a historic palazzo.
➕ F4 ✉ Via de' Ginori 21r ☎ 055 260 8659 🚌 1, 6, 7, 10, 11, 17

ZANOBINI
Part traditional bar, part wine shop, Zanobini's is patronzied by locals. Stop by for a drink and a snack while you buy your wine.
➕ F4 ✉ Via Sant'Antonino 47r ☎ 055 239 6850 🚌 11, A

Entertainment and Nightlife

ASTOR CAFFÈ
Stylish café/bar serving up Mediterranean dishes accompanied by house, jazz and easy-listening soundtrack. Grab a seat for an *apertivo* and munch on the buffet snacks before the DJ gets going in the back room.
🔲 F5 ✉ Piazza Duomo 20r ☎ 055 239 9000 🚍 1, 14, 23, A

JAZZ CLUB
www.jazzclubfirenze.it
A popular venue among jazz aficionados. Although technically a private club, it is very easy to become a member (▷ panel). If you like live jazz and a relaxed atmosphere, then this is the place for you.
🔲 H5 ✉ Via Nuova dei Caccini 3 ☎ 055 247 9700 🕐 Closed Mon, Sun and Jun–Sep 🚍 C

LYCEUM
www.lyceumclubfirenze.net
This multicultural organization presents an occasional schedule of chamber music and classical recitals in elegant surroundings.
🔲 G5 ✉ Via degli Alfani 48r ☎ 055 247 8264 🚍 1, 6, 7, 10, 11, 17

OPERA ET GUSTO
This is a novel way to spend an evening, combining a first-class meal with music, dance and theatre. The tables are arranged at the foot of the stage and red velvet curtains encircle

the room creating an intimate, warm feel. After the performance the venue transforms into an open bar with live music.
🔲 E5 ✉ Via della Scala 17r ☎ 055 288 190 🕐 Show 8pm–10.45pm. Bar until 2am 🚍 6, 11, 12, 36, A

PALESTRA RICCIARDI
www.palestraricciardi.it
The oldest, biggest and most central gym in the city, founded some 50 years ago, with all the latest equipment.
🔲 H4 ✉ Borgo Pinti 75 🕐 055 247 8444 🚍 6, 31, 32, C

CLUBS ITALIAN STYLE
Many clubs and music venues (and even a few bars and restaurants) are private clubs or *associazione culturale*. This doesn't mean that visitors are unwelcome but rather that it's easier for them to get a licence as a club than as a public *locale*. It's really very easy to become a member; you may be charged a euro or so over and above the official entry price, but it's still worth doing even if you're only going to use your membership once. Many clubs actually have free membership. All you need to do is fill in your name, address, date of birth and sometimes occupation on a form and you'll be presented with a membership card.

REX CAFÈ
A popular bar with a spellbinding interior of retro lighting and paint-splashed walls. Open until 2.30am.
🔲 H5 ✉ Via Fiesolana 23r ☎ 055 248 0331 🚍 14, 23, A, C

SPACE ELECTRONIC
www.spaceelectronic.net
Upstairs you'll find a vast dance floor, where a huge variety of music is played, from up-to-the-minute hits to 1950s and 60s classics. Noisy and very popular with tourists.
🔲 D5 ✉ Via Palazzuolo 37 ☎ 055 293 082 🚍 36, 37, D

TEATRO COMUNALE
The largest of Florence's concert halls—the main venue of the Maggio Musicale in spring and the festival's box office—also has its own classical season. The Ridotto, or Piccolo, is the theatre's smaller auditorium.
🔲 C5 ✉ Corso Italia 16 ☎ Box office 055 287 222 🚍 B

TEATRO DELLA PERGOLA
www.pergola.firenze.it
Well-known productions are regularly held in the sumptuous surroundings of the two elegant halls. An important venue for classical music, with some Maggio Musicale concerts held here.
🔲 G5 ✉ Via della Pergola 12–32 ☎ 055 22641 🚍 14, 23, C

Restaurants

PRICES

Prices are approximate, based on a 3-course meal for one person.

€€€	over €45
€€	€20–€45
€	under €20

BELCORE (€€)

www.ristorantebelcore.it
Enjoy refined modern Italian cooking in tranquil, elegant surroundings. The plain cream walls provide a stage for the work of up-and-coming artists. There is an impressive wine list with more than 300 wines to choose from.
➕ D5 ✉ Via dell'Albero 30 ☎ 055 211 198 ⏰ Closed lunch Tue, Wed 🚋 1, 2, 9, 16 17, A

CANTINETTA ANTINORI (€€€)

www.cantinetta-antinori.com
A refined setting for the chic Florentine elite. The food comes from the farm of the Antinori family, whose wines are world renowned. The wonderful dishes use the best seasonal produce. Dress up or you are likely to feel completely out of place.
➕ E5 ✉ Piazza Antinori 3 ☎ 055 292 234 ⏰ Closed Sat, Sun, Aug 🚋 6, 11, 37, A

COQUINARIUS (€€)

This restaurant-cum-wine bar full of dark wood and stylish posters is a great place to sample different cheeses, cold cuts, smoked fish, *carpacci* meats and *stuzzichini* (Italian bar snacks), and exceptionally good cakes.
➕ F5 ✉ Via delle Oche 15r ☎ 055 230 2153 ⏰ Closed Sun 🚋 14, 23, A

GELATERIA CARABÉ (€)

www.gelatocarabe.com
A top-quality Sicilian ice cream store run with great pride by Antonio and Loredana Lisciandro. *The* place to have a *granita* (ice slush) in Florence, or try the *cremolata* made from the fruit pulp, including melon and blackberry. No artificial ingredients are added to the products.
➕ G4 ✉ Via Ricasoli 60r ☎ 055 289 476 🚋 14, 23, C

LA GIOSTRA (€€€)

www.ristorantelagiostra.com
Prepare to be spoiled at this enclave of fine dining, owned by a Hapsburg

ITALIAN CAKES

There are three main types of Italian cake. *Brioche* (pastries) are made with sweet yeast dough and filled with oozing custard. *Torte* (cakes) tend to be tarts, such as the ubiquitous *torta della nonna* (granny's cake), a kind of cake in tart form, or *torta di ricotta*, in which ricotta is mixed with sugar and candied peel. Then there are all kinds of little cookies, most of which contain nuts and have names like *brutti ma buoni* (ugly but good).

prince and run by his daughter and twin sons. Upon entering, you are offered a crystal flute of *spumante*, which prepares you for the refined menu. The home-made pasta courses are divine and the mains are equally imaginative and exquisite. Save room for the Viennese *sacher torte*. Twinkling lights decorate the cosy dining room, which is surmounted by 16th-century brick arches.
➕ G5 ✉ Borgo Pinti 10r ☎ 055 241 341 🚋 6, 31, C

✰GOZZI SERGIO (€)

A basic but good trattoria with a daily changing menu. Hidden behind the Mercato San Lorenzo, it is not the easiest place to find and it's only open for lunch, but it's worth a detour.
➕ F5 ✉ Piazza San Lorenzo 8r ☎ 055 281 941 ⏰ Closed dinner, Sun, Aug 🚋 1, 6, 17, 23

LE MOSSACCE (€–€€)

www.trattorialemossacce.it
Bustling eatery between the Duomo and the Bargello. Excellent Tuscan food including rich soup.
➕ G6 ✉ Via del Proconsolo 55r ☎ 055 294 361 ⏰ Closed Sat, Sun, Aug 🚋 14, 23, A

PALLE D'ORO (€)

Spotless and spartan, this restaurant serves good food and is excellent value. Expect hearty soups, gnocchi dumpling

dishes, decent fish and filling pasta servings. Adequate wine list.
🔹 F4 ✉ Via Sant'Antonino 27r ☎ 055 288 383 🕐 Closed Sun 🚌 1, 7, 10

RELAIS LE JARDIN (€€€)

The dark wood and carpeted interiors, and the lush well-kept gardens give the Hotel Regency's restaurant a British feel. Immaculately prepared and presented menu. Reserve early to ensure a candlelit table.
🔹 H5 ✉ Piazza Massimo D'Azeglio ☎ 055 245 247 🚌 6, 31, 32, C

ROBIGLIO (€€)

www.robiglio.it
The old-fashioned Florentine bar/*pasticceria* par excellence opened its first branch in 1928. The pastries are to die for.
🔹 F5 ✉ Via Tosinghi 11r ☎ 055 215 013 🚌 A

RUTH'S (€)

www.kosheruth.com
A bright, modern Jewish restaurant next to the synagogue serving an interesting mix of vegetarian (although fish is also served), Middle Eastern and kosher food.
🔹 H5 ✉ Via Farini 2a ☎ 055 248 0888 🕐 Closed Fri dinner, Sat lunch 🚌 6, 31, 32, C

SABATINI (€€€)

www.ristorantesabatini.it
This elegant, wood-filled restaurant is a respected

Florentine stalwart. Particularly good for local steak and excellent seafood risotto.
🔹 E5 ✉ Via dei Panzani 9a ☎ 055 282 802 🕐 Closed Mon 🚌 1, 7, 11, 22, 36, 37, A

TAVERNA DEL BRONZINO (€€–€€€)

Here you will find a wealth of Tuscan culinary delights such as smoked goose breast with olive oil. If available, and you love fish, try the expertly prepared sea bass. Expect excellent service.
🔹 F3 ✉ Via delle Route 25r ☎ 055 495 220 🕐 Closed Sun, Aug 🚌 12, 20

TRATTORIA ANTELLESI (€€)

www.trattoriaantellesi.com
A great place for a vegetarian to join a meat-eating friend. Good range

of inventive starters and delicious main courses— the *peposo alla fiorentina* (a peppery beef stew in red wine) is very tasty. There is a decent wine list and a traditional Florentine dessert made with chestnuts.
🔹 E4 ✉ Via Faenza 9r ☎ 055 216 990 🕐 Closed Tue 🚌 12, 25, 33

TRATTORIA ANTICHI CANCELLI (€)

Hearty Tuscan food served at this mainstay trattoria. There is a good selection for vegetarians on the mixed menu, including hearty soups, *contorni* (side dishes) and the classic spaghetti *pomodoro e basilico* (tomato and basil). Good value house wine.
🔹 E4 ✉ Via Faenza 73r ☎ 055 218 927 🕐 Closed Mon 🚌 12, 25, 33

ZÀ-ZÀ (€–€€)

www.trattoriazaza.it
An old-fashioned, inexpensive trattoria near the Mercato Centrale, which is very popular with visitors. The Tuscan food is excellent, and the fixed-price menus are great value. The inviting stone-walled interior is especially appealing in the summer heat. It's best to arrive at opening time or reserve a table.
🔹 F4 ✉ Piazza del Mercato Centrale 26r ☎ 055 215 411 🕐 Closed Sun (except last Sun of month) 🚌 12, 25, 33

Literally translated as 'beyond the Arno', the Oltrarno is the site of the Pitti Palace and the Boboli Gardens. It is also the most relaxed part of the city, least touched by tourism and with some of the best views.

4

5

6

LUNGARNO SODERINI
Piazza
di Cestello
San Frediano
in Cestello
Piazza
N Sauro
BORGO SAN FREDIANO
LUNGARNO GUICCIARDINI
Via
Chiesa
S Presb
Piazza
Frescobaldi
Palazzo
Frescobaldi
Piazza del
Carmine
Piazza del
Borgo d stella
SANTO
SPIRITO
Via di Leone
**Cappella
Brancacci**
Santa Maria
del Carmine
Via s Monaca
Via dell'Ardiglione
Via S Agostino
Via
**Santo
Spirito**
Spirito Santo
Borgo S Jacopo
Palazzo
Firidolfi
Via de Guicciardini
Piazza
di Santa
Felicita
Piazza
d Rossi
Piazza di
Santa Maria
Soprarno
VIA
della
Piazza
S Spirito
El Presso di Marino
Maggio
Via Sguazza
**Santa
Felicita**
Via
7

_Giardino
Torrigiani_
VIALE FRANCESCO
Via della Chiesa
Via delle Caldaie
Via Mazzetta
Via Toscanella
Palazzo
Corsini
Via Romana
Piazza
de' Pitti
**Palazzo
Pitti**
**Galleria del
Costume**
San
Girolamo
Santo
Spirito
Via
della
Costa
Via di Santa Maria
Campuccio
Via Santa Maria
Borgo
Palazzo
Torrigiani
Piazza
S Felice
**Galleria d'Arte
Moderna**
Vicolo della Cava
Via dello Sdrucciolo
Costa San Giorgio
8

VIA DE SERRAGLI
**Museo della
Specola**
Giardino
di Bòboli
Viale dei Cipressi
Fontana
del Nettuno
**Museo delle
Porcellane**
**Forte di
Belvedere**
VIA PETRARCA
Porta
Romana
Piazzale di
Porta Romana
Istituto
d'Arte
V d Madonna
Via di Macchiaoli
Via del Baluardo
d Pace
S Leonardo
in Arcetri
Via di San Leonardo
BOBOLINO
Via del Bobolino
9

VIALE NICCOLÒ MACHIAVELLI

0 —— 250 m
0 —— 250 yds

C   **D**   **E**   **F**

Lungarno Torrigiani

Ponte alle Grazie

Arno

Ch Evangelica Luterana

Palazzo Serristori

LUNGARNO

Piazza d'MOZZI

Via dei Renai

Museo Bardini

Via del Giardino Serristori

SERRISTORI

LUNGARNO B CELLINI

Porta San Niccolò

Via d Fornace

Palazzo Torrigiani

Via

San Niccolò

Piazza G Poggi

Via dei Bastioni

Palazzi de' Mozzi

San Niccolò

SAN NICCOLÒ

Via di Belvedere

Giuseppe Poggi

Viale

Camping Michelangelo

David

Via d Monte alle Croci

Piazzale Michelangelo

VIALE MICHELANGIOLO

Via di San Miniato al Monte

Via

San Salvatore al Monte

dell'Erta

Convento delle Stimmatine

Via del Mte alle croci

Canina

GALILEI

Viuzzo della Corta

Giramonte

San Miniato al Monte

GALILEO

Cimitero delle Porte Sante

Via delle Porte

Passo all'Erta

VIALE

Viuzzo al Gelata

Via dei

G   **H**   **J**

Cappella Brancacci

Part of the thrill of the Cappella Brancacci is observing in Masaccio's frescoes the power of expression and technical brilliance that inspired the Florentine painters of the 15th century.

Minature gem This tiny chapel is reached via the cloisters of the otherwise rather dull Santa Maria del Carmine. Two layers of frescoes commissioned in 1424 by Felice Brancacci, a wealthy Florentine merchant and statesman, illustrate the life of St. Peter, shown in his orange gown. The frescoes were designed by Masolino da Panicale, who began painting them with his brilliant pupil, Masaccio. In 1428 Masaccio took over from Masolino but died that year, aged 27; the rest of the frescoes were completed in the 1480s by Filippino Lippi.

Restoration revelations In the 1980s the chapel was restored, with the removal of accumulated candle soot and layers of an 18th-century egg-based gum (which had formed a mould). The frescoes now have an intense radiance that makes it possible to see very clearly the shifts in emphasis between Masolino's work and that of Masaccio; contrast the serenity of Masolino's *Temptation of Adam and Eve* with the excruciating agony of Masaccio's *Expulsion of Adam and Eve from Paradise*. The restoration has also highlighted Masaccio's mastery of chiaroscuro (light and shade), which, combined with his grasp of perspective, was marvelled at and consciously copied by 15th-century Florentine painters.

THE BASICS

www.museicivicifiorentini.it/brancacci

✚ D6

✉ Santa Maria del Carmine, Piazza del Carmine (enter through the cloisters)

☎ 055 238 2195; 055 276 8224 (reservations)

🕐 Mon, Wed–Sat 10–5, Sun 1–5. Entrance by reservation only

🚌 6, D

♿ Poor

✋ Moderate

HIGHLIGHTS

● Masaccio's *Expulsion of Adam and Eve from Paradise*
● Masaccio's *St. Peter heals the Sick*
● Filippino Lippi's *St. Paul visits St. Peter in Prison*
● Masaccio's *Tribute Money*

OLTRARNO

★

TOP 25

Giardino di Boboli

Views and fountains abound in the Boboli Gardens, a welcome haven

The Boboli Gardens are, quite literally, a breath of fresh air. They are the only easily accessible reservoir of greenery and tranquillity in Florence, and a lovely retreat after a hard day's sightseeing.

Renaissance origins The Boboli Gardens were created for the Medici when they moved to the Palazzo Pitti in 1550. They represent a superb example of Italian Renaissance gardening, an interplay between nature and artifice expressed in a geometrical arrangement of fountains, grass and low box hedges. In 1766 they were opened to the public, and in 1992 an (unpopular) entrance charge was imposed.

Amphitheatre Just behind the Palazzo Pitti is the amphitheatre, built where the stone for the palazzo was quarried. It was the site of the first-ever opera performance and is surrounded by mazelike alleys of fragrant, dusty bay trees. Go uphill past the Neptune Fountain (1565–68) to reach the Giardino dei Cavalieri, where roses and peonies wilt in the summer sun. The pretty building nearby houses the Museo delle Porcellane (Porcelain Museum, ▷ 86).

More to see The Viottolone, an avenue of cypresses planted in 1637 and studded with classical statues, leads to the Isolotto, an island set in a murky green pond dotted with pleasantly crumbling statues. In the middle is a copy of Giambologna's *Oceanus* fountain (1576), the original of which is in the Bargello (▷ 24–25).

Crowds flock up the steps of San Miniato al Monte to view its glorious mosaics

TOP 25 San Miniato al Monte

San Miniato is a wonderful sight on the hill above Florence, its marble facade glistening in the sunlight. Close up it is even more appealing, a jewel of the Romanesque inside and outside.

Christian martyr San Miniato (St. Minias) was an early Christian martyr who came to Florence from the Levant in the third century and was martyred in the Roman amphitheatre that stood on the site of today's Piazza della Signoria, by order of the Emperor Decius. It is said that his decapitated body picked up his head and walked into the hills. His shrine, the site of the present church, was built where he finally collapsed. The church was initially run by Benedictine monks, then by Cluniacs, and finally, from 1373 to the present day, by the Olivetans. In the Benedictine shop, on the right as you exit, monks sell honey and herbal potions.

An eagle visitation The church was built in 1018, with a green-and-white marble facade added at the end of the 11th century and mosaics in the 13th century. On the pinnacle a gilded copper statue of an eagle carries a bale of cloth (1410): This is the symbol of the Arte di Calimala, the wool importers' guild, which supported the church in the Middle Ages.

Miraculous crucifix Inside, an inlaid floor (c1207) incorporates zodiac and animal themes. In the nave is a chapel (1448) by Michelozzo, built to house a miraculous crucifix that is now in Santa Trinità.

THE BASICS

✚ H9

✉ Via Monte alle Croce, off Viale Galileo Galilei

☎ 055 234 2731

🕐 Apr–end Oct daily 8–7; Nov–end Mar 8–12, 3–6; closed during services

🚌 12, 13

♿ Poor (make enquires)

🎫 Free

HIGHLIGHTS

● Marble facade
● Inlaid floor
● Mosaics in the apse
● Cappella del Crocifisso
● Wooden ceiling
● Cardinal of Portugal Chapel (1473)

OLTRARNO

★

TOP 25

Palazzo Pitti

TOP 25

HIGHLIGHTS

● Frescoed ceilings by Pietro da Cortona, Galleria Palatina
● Raphael's *Madonna of the Chair* (c1516)
● Titian's overtly sexual *Mary Magdalene* (c1531)
● Van Dyck's *Charles I and Henrietta Maria* (c1632)
● Titian's *Portrait of a Gentleman* (1540)

TIPS

● It makes sense to concentrate on the Galleria Palatina before moving on to another gallery.
● Be prepared for crowds, and sections to be closed.
● Book ahead to avoid disappointment.
● Leave time to relax afterwards in the Giardino di Boboli (▷ 82). Combined tickets can be bought.

The Pitti Palace, with its four museums, is unremittingly grand, opulent and pompous. Its saving grace is the outstanding collection of Renaissance and baroque art in the Galleria Palatina.

Bigger and better The Palazzo Pitti was built in 1457 to designs by Filippo Brunelleschi for banker Luca Pitti. He wanted it to be bigger and better than the Medici Palace. The result has been likened to a 'rusticated Stalinist ministry'. Ironically, the Medici bought the Palazzo Pitti in 1550 when the Pitti lost their fortune, and it became the residence of the rulers of Florence.

Great art The Galleria Palatina contains baroque and Renaissance works from the Medici collection as important as those in the Uffizi (▷ 28–29).

Clockwise from left: Cortona's ceiling fresco in the Sala di Marte inside th[e] Pitti's Palatine Gallery depicts the Roman God of War; the home of the M[edici] for three centuries, the imposing Palazzo Pitti was designed in 1458 and [extended in] the 16th century; Palazzo Pitti seen from Giardino di Bobli

Highlights include masterpieces by Titian, Raphael and Van Dyck displayed in a haphazard way that reflects the taste of the Medici, who had so many works of art that they didn't worry about hanging them in any order. The Appartamenti Reali (State Rooms) are entered through the gallery.

Over the top The Museo degli Argenti (Silver Museum) is a triumph of Medici wealth over taste. Rooms are full of ghoulish reliquaries, Roman glass and Roman and Byzantine vases in *pietra dura* style (inlaid with marble and semiprecious stones) that belonged to Lorenzo the Magnificent. Upstairs is a display of cameos, as well as a 17th-century glass Crucifixion scene that is in such appalling taste as to be hilarious. The other two museums are the Galleria del Costume (▷ 86) and the Galleria d'Arte Moderna (▷ 86).

THE BASICS

www.polomuseale.firenze.it
✚ E7
✉ Piazza Pitti
☎ Galleria Palatina 055 238 8614; Argenti 055 238 8709
🕐 Galleria Palatina Tue–Sun 8.15–6.50; closed Jan. Argenti (▷ 82; same as Giardino di Boboli)
🚍 11, 36, 37, D
♿ Good
📖 Galleria Palatina, Royal Apartments; Galleria d'Arte Moderna combined ticket expensive; Museo degli Argenti (▷ 82, Boboli Gardens)

More to See

FORTE DI BELVEDERE
This was built by the Medici in 1590 as a refuge for the Medici Grand Dukes in their struggle against the Florentine Republic, and as a reminder of Medici military might. Occasional exhibitions are held here.
➕ F8 ✉ Via San Leonardo ☎ 055 262 5962 🚹 View from the road 🚌 D, C, plus walk 🖐 Free

GALLERIA D'ARTE MODERNA
www.polomuseale.firenze.it
More than 30 rooms of artworks here span the mid-18th to mid-20th century. In the main building of the Palazzo Pitti on the floor above the Palatina.
➕ E7 ✉ Palazzo Pitti, Piazza Pitti ☎ 055 238 8616 🚹 Tue–Sun 8.15–6.50 🚌 11, 36, 37, D ♿ Good 🎟 Inclusive ticket with Galleria Palatina (▷ 84) expensive

GALLERIA DEL COSTUME
www.polomuseale.firenze.it
One for devotees to clothes and fashion. The collection illustrates the history of costume from the 18th century up to the 1920s. Displays change frequently, and the gallery hosts many special exhibitions. In the Palazzina Meridiana in the south wing of the Palazzo Pitti.
➕ E7 ✉ Palazzo Pitti, Piazza Pitti ☎ 055 238 8713 🚹 Giardino di Boboli (▷ 82, panel) 🚌 11, 36, 37, D ♿ Good 🎟 Inclusive ticket with Museo degli Argenti, Museo delle Porcellane, Giardino di Boboli expensive

MUSEO DELLA SPECOLA
La Specola is so called after the observatory that used to be sited here. The museum of zoology and natural history is part of the university. An unusual highlight is the Cere Anatomiche, a gruesome set of 18th-century wax models of bits of human bodies. Also hundreds of skeletons and stuffed animals are on show.
➕ E7 ✉ Via Romana 17 ☎ 055 228 8251 🚹 Tue–Sun 9.30–4.30 🚌 11, 36, D ♿ Good 🖐 Expensive

MUSEO DELLE PORCELLANE
www.polomuseale.firenze.it
French, Italian, German and Viennese

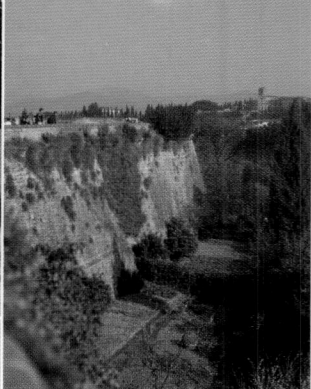

Museo delle Porcellane

Defensive position—Forte di Belvedere

porcelain and ceramics in a pavilion at the top of the Giardino di Boboli. ✚ E8 ✉ Giardino di Boboli, Piazza Pitti 🕾 055 238 8709 🕓 Giardino di Boboli (▷ 82, panel) 🚌 11, 36, 37, D ⛬ Good, some steps ✋ Inclusive ticket Museo degli Argenti, Museo delle Porcellane, Giardino di Boboli expensive

PIAZZALE MICHELANGELO

Despite the fact that Piazzale Michelangelo is frequented by bus-loads of tourists, this stupendous vantage point is still very much worth the trip, either by bus or on foot. Ignore the poor green copy of Michelangelo's *David* and crop of souvenir stalls, beware of pickpockets and soak up the wonderful view. ✚ H8 ✉ Viale Galileo Galilei 🚌 12, 13 ⛬ Good ✋ Free

PONTE ALLE GRAZIE

Dating from 1237, when it was known as Ponte Rubaconte (the bridge over the River Rubicon), then rebuilt after World War II to a modern design. Its name is from the oratory of Santa Maria delle Grazie, which once stood here. ✚ G7 🚌 23, C, D

SANTA FELICITA

This is the second-oldest church in Florence, dating to the second century AD, when Syrian and Greek merchants settled here. The highlight is the Mannerist *Deposition* (1525–28) by Pontormo, in the Cappella Caponi, immediately on your right as you enter. It is a stunning vortex of improbable forms and hues: lime green, bubblegum pink, acid yellow. ✚ F7 ✉ Piazza Santa Felicita 🕾 055 213 018 🕓 Mon–Sat 9–12, 3.30–5.30. Closed Sun and during services. Mass: Sun 9, 11, Mon–Sat 6pm 🚌 D ⛬ Poor ✋ Free

SANTO SPIRITO

Designed by Filippo Brunelleschi in 1435, with an 18th-century baroque facade, which was never finished. The *cenacolo* (refectory) houses a fresco of the *Last Supper* by Nardo di Clone. ✚ E7 ✉ Piazza Santo Spirito 🕾 055 210 030 🕓 Thu–Tue 10–12.30, 4–5.30 (not during services) 🚌 D ⛬ Poor ✋ Free

Get a great view from Piazzale Michelangelo

Around Oltrarno

Begin amid the bustle of Oltrarno, yet you're soon among tranquil surroundings to catch a glimpse of local life and see great views.

DISTANCE: 2km (1 mile) **ALLOW:** 2–3 hours

START

PONTE VECCHIO (▷ 34)
✚ F7 🚌 B, D

END

PIAZZALE MICHELANGELO (▷ 87)
✚ H8 🚌 12, 13

① In summer this walk can be baking hot; start early in the morning or after 4pm and take a bottle of water. Plan a midday picnic at the Forte di Belvedere (▷ 86).

② Set off from the south side of the Ponte Vecchio (▷ 34–35) in Oltrarno. With your back to the bridge, take the first square on your left, Piazza di Santa Felicita.

③ Here you will find Pontormo's *Deposition* in Santa Felicita (▷ 87) church. Take the road on the left of the church, the Costa di San Giorgio, where Galileo lived at No. 19.

④ Continue up its steep slope. At the top, you pass through Porta di San Giorgio (1260), the oldest city gate, with a carving of St. George slaying the dragon.

⑧ Continue downhill to Piazzale Michelangelo for great views. A No. 12 bus will take you back down to Ponte alle Grazie (▷ 87).

⑦ A little way up take the steep Via di San Salvadore al Monte on the left, which crosses Viale Galileo Galilei. Climb the hill flanked by cypress trees that continues up toward San Miniato (▷ 83). Return to Viale Galileo Galilei and go right.

⑥ After the entrance to Fort Belvedere, descend steeply along the 13th-century defensive city walls. At the bottom of the hill, by the small gateway of Porta San Miniato, turn right and head up Via del Monte alle Croci.

⑤ Follow Via del Belvedere, and leave the 1590 Forte di Belvedere on your right.

Shopping

ALCOZER & J
www.alcozer.it
Sells quirky stylish pieces in a modern idiom using interesting metals and bright stones; costume brooches, necklaces and other items of jewellery.
➕ E7 ✉ Via Mannelli 15r ☎ 055 623 6346 🚌 D

ANNA
www.annapitti.it
This shop is in a 300-year-old tower in front of the Pitti Palace. Anna sells a great range of leather goods, bags, knitwear, cashmere, scarves and ties. A good place for men and women to shop in a quieter part of town.
➕ E7 ✉ Piazza Pitti 38–40r ☎ 055 283 787 🚌 36, 37, D

ANTICO SETIFICIO FIORENTINO
www.setificiofiorentino.it
Ring the doorbell to gain access to this old Florentine silk factory that provides fabric for some of Italy's most sought-after designers. Much of the fabric is woven using traditional methods and 18th-century looms.
➕ C6 ✉ Via Lorenzo Bartolini 4 ☎ 055 213 861 🚌 D

BARTOLOZZI & MAIOLI
This antiques shop gives an insight into the Florentine love of ostentatious adornment. As you wander you can hear craftsmen tapping. Good pieces, but expensive.

➕ E7 ✉ Via Maggio 13r ☎ 055 239 8633 🚌 11, 36, 37, D

BOTTEGA DEL MOSAICO
www.bottegadelmosaico.com
The art of the Florentine mosaic, an inlay of hard and semiprecious stones, is unique in the world. The art has been practised for more than 500 years and it flourished at the court of the Medicis. Stones used range from agate to malachite. Examples can be seen in the world's top museums including the Uffizi Gallery (▷ 28–29).
➕ E7 ✉ Via Guicciardini 126r ☎ 055 210 718 🚌 36, 37, D

POTTERY FACTS

Traditional Italian ceramics are majolica, terracotta covered with a brilliant tin-based glaze. Arabic ceramics inspired pots made for the Medici court at Montelupo, near Florence. Deruta in Umbria makes flowery designs in blue on white or yellow. Designs in turquoise on white are also much in evidence. Tuscan peasant wares, white or yellow, splashed with green or blue spots, are increasingly popular. Among the best-known classic designs is Gran Faenza, with green, red and blue floral designs on a pale grey-blue background. Most shops offer shipping.

BOTTEGA DELLE STAMPE
www.bottegadellestampa.com
Framed and unframed antique or art nouveau prints (known in Italian as Liberty). Elegant.
➕ E6 ✉ Borgo San Jacopo 56r ☎ 055 295 396 🚌 D

LA CASA DELLA STAMPA
Vivianna is the lithographer who hand-tints many of these beautiful prints. There is a huge selection of Florentine scenes, from the Medici era to the early 19th century, and richly painted studies of butterflies and plants.
➕ E7 ✉ Sdrucciolo de Pitti 11r ☎ No phone 🚌 11, 36, 37, D

ENOTECA PERI
A no-nonsense wine and oil shop selling quality products. Just over the Santa Trinità bridge.
➕ E7 ✉ Via Maggio 5r ☎ 055 212 674 🚌 11, 36, D

FARMACIA PITTI
It's worth walking through this former 15th-century herbalist shop just to see the sales room at the back decked out with antique glass jars and old cabinets. A modern working pharmacy serves your needs, too.
➕ E7 ✉ Piazza San Felice 4r ☎ 055 224 402 🚌 6, D

GALLERIA PONTE VECCHIO
Tucked away down a narrow alleyway off Via

Guicciardini, this pretty little shop is full to the brim with brightly coloured Italian ceramics, which are guaranteed to cheer up your home.
➕ E7 ✉ Via Guicciardini 104r ☎ 055 239 400 🚍 36, 37, D

GIOVANNI TURCHI

This huge trove of period pieces is well worth delving into. The store has been in the family for years, and has a huge amount of stock from the local area, Venice and the Veneto. Pieces are less expensive than they would be back home.
➕ E7 ✉ Via Maggio 50–54r ☎ 055 217 341 🚍 36, 37, D

GIULIO GIANNINI E FIGLIO

www.giuliogiannini.it
The best-known of Florence's stationery shops, established in 1856, sells tasteful cards and books bound in leather, as well as beautifully finished desktop paraphernalia, letter racks and pen holders, all covered with marbled paper.
➕ E7 ✉ Piazza Pitti 37r ☎ 055 212 621 🚍 36, 37, D

J. T. CASINI

www.casinifirenze.it
The latest in Italian and international designer clothing for women. Up-and-coming designers are showcased alongside well-known, prestigious brands.
➕ E7 ✉ Piazza Pitti 30–31r ☎ 055 219 324 🚍 36, 37, D

MADOVA GLOVES

www.madova.com/shop
A staggering array of fine gloves lined with silk, cashmere and fur in every hue. Family run; established in 1919.
➕ E7 ✉ Via Guicciardini 1r ☎ 055 239 6526 🚍 36, 37, D

MOLERIA LOCCHI

www.locchi.com
This shop, next to the Prato dello Strozzino, sells the most extraordinary glass you will see outside Venice created using authentic, traditional methods.
➕ C7 ✉ Via Domenico Burchiello 10 ☎ 055 229 8371 🚍 C, D

OLIO & CONVIVIUM

www.conviviumfirenze.it
This pristine delicatessen ensures its first-class

quality products respect local traditions. Bakery goods, cheeses, charcuterie and other fresh produce are beautifully displayed beside a huge range of olive oils and wine. There's an adjoining restaurant.
➕ E6 ✉ Via Santo Spirito 4 ☎ 055 265 8198 🚍 11, 36, 37, D

PITTI BOUTIQUE

The wisdom and creativity of fine craftsmanship combine to make elegant and beautifully finished cashmere in brilliant and natural hues.
➕ E7 ✉ Via dello Sprone 13r ☎ 055 280 285 🚍 11, 36, 37, D

RIVE GAUCHE

www.rivegaucheshoes.com
Many people visit Florence to buy leather and especially shoes. This shop takes you back in time with its handmade shoes and boots in gorgeous Italian leather.
➕ E7 ✉ Via Guicciardini 31r ☎ 055 213 474 🚍 D

IL TORCHIO

www.legatorioiltorchio.com
As you walk into this stationery shop you are instantly aware that this is a place where things are made, not just a showroom. You can buy sheets of marbled paper or have it made up to suit your requirements. There are also ready-made marbled paper goods available.
➕ F7 ✉ Via dei Bardi 17 ☎ 055 234 2862 🚍 C, D

CAFFÈ RICCHI

This trendy Oltrarno bar is a good place to have coffee during the day, but it really only comes alive at night, especially in the summer, when you can sit outside.

➕ E7 ✉ Piazza Santo Spirito 9r ☎ 055 215 864 🚫 Closed Sun 🚌 11, 36, 37, D

CAVALLI CLUB

www.cavalliclub.com
Seeing is believing here, with typical Cavalli-style opulence and the inevitable animal prints throughout. Upstairs there is a restaurant, downstairs a stunning bar with a dance floor lowered after midnight. Opens at 7pm every night.

➕ D6 ✉ Piazza del Carmine 8r ☎ 055 211 650 🚌 D

DRINKING LAWS

The legal age for buying alcohol in bars or shops is 18. Opening times for licensed premises are not set, although there are restrictions before, during and after some football (soccer) matches. Laws against drinking and driving are firmly enforced.

LA DOLCE VITA

www.dolcevitaflorence.com
This is one of the hippest places for young Florentines to hang out. A great place for an *aperitivo* and to mingle with the preclub *bella gente*. It stays open until 2am.

➕ D6 ✉ Piazza del Carmine 6r ☎ 055 284 595 🚌 6, D

HEMINGWAY

www.hemingway.fi.it
Chic, funky café and bar with light meals, great cocktails, specialty teas, fine coffees and chocolates, just off Piazza del Carmine. Stays open until 2am on Friday and Saturday.

➕ D6 ✉ Piazza Piattellina 9r ☎ 055 284 781 🚌 6, D

UNIVERSALE

www.universalefirenze.it
This former cinema space is now dedicated to dance music, cocktail drinking and Italian food. Mid-week focuses on commercial house while Saturday night sees a more eclectic music policy—funk, jazz and exotica.

➕ C6 ✉ Via Pisana 77r ☎ 055 221 122 🚫 Closed Mon, Tue, Wed 🚌 6, 12

Restaurants

PRICES

Prices are approximate, based on a 3-course meal for one person.

€€€	over €45
€€	€20–€45
€	under €20

AL TRANVAI (€)

www.altranvai.it
Diners are packed into this lively trattoria on the same square as the weekly market. Popular (with locals) is *frattaglie* (a mind-boggling range of offal) but the menu changes every day.

➕ C7 ✉ Piazza Torquato Tasso 14r ☎ 055 225 197 🚫 Closed Sun 🚌 12, 13

CAFFÈ PITTI (€–€€)

www.caffepitti.it
Just the place for a break in a perfect setting opposite the Palazzo Pitti. You can have breakfast, light lunch, tea or coffee any time. Have a predinner cocktail then a pleasant meal viewing the flood-lighted palazzo. Specialty of the house are the hand-picked unique truffles from the natural reserve owned by the Caffè Pitti, used to create some special dishes.

➕ E7 ✉ Piazza Pitti 9 ☎ 055 239 9863 🚌 6, D

CAMMILLO (€€–€€€)

A well-established trattoria that attracts an international crowd and a host of Italian celebrities enticed by the excellent home-made pasta, various *baccalà* (salted cod) dishes and expertly cooked meats. Try some of the Masiero family's virgin olive oil with bread. Great choice of Tuscan and Piedmontese wines.

➕ E6 ✉ Borgo San Jacopo 57r ☎ 055 212 427 🕐 Closed Wed 🚍 11, 36, D

IL CANTINONE (€–€€)

www.ilcantinonedifirenze.it
This restaurant is in an arched cellar. Long communal tables add a party atmosphere. Good wholesome fare.

➕ E7 ✉ Via de San Spirito 6r ☎ 055 218 898 🕐 Closed Mon 🚍 11, 36, 37, D

LA CASALINGA (€–€€)

A busy family-run place that is a good place to try *ribollita*, the Florentine soup made with bread and vegetables.

➕ B8 ✉ Via dei Michelozzi 9r ☎ 055 218 624 🕐 Closed Sun 🚍 11, 36, D

MARACANA GRILL (€€)

www.maracanagrill.com
For something completely different, just steps away from the Piazza Santo Spirito, try this restaurant dedicated to the flavours of Brazil. The decor is bright and fun and the food spot on, particularly for carnivores.

➕ E7 ✉ Borgo Tegolaio 17r ☎ 055 238 2290 🕐 Closed Mon 🚍 11, 36, 37, D

OSTERIA DEL CINGHIALE BIANCO (€€)

The White Boar is named after one of Tuscany's greatest culinary special-ties. Don't worry, there are chicken, veal and rabbit dishes as well.

➕ E6 ✉ Borgo San Jacopo 43r ☎ 055 215 706 🕐 Closed Wed dinner 🚍 11, 36, D

OSTERIA SANTO SPIRITO (€€)

A delightful trattoria with outdoor seating and a menu of robust main courses and pasta dishes such as oven-baked

---

CONTRADICTION

The concept of vegetarianism is not one that sits easily with Italian ideas about food, and there are very few vegetarian restaurants in Italy. However, there are few better coun-tries for those who do not eat meat (or fish). Many pasta dishes contain no meat—pesto, tomato sauce or ravioli stuffed with spinach and ricotta, to name but a few. For a main course, try *grigliata di verdura* (grilled vegetables) or else restaurant stalwarts such as *parmigiana di melanzane* (aubergine [eggplant] layered with tomato and mozzarella, and baked with a Parmesan crust), *mozzarella in carrozza* (fried mozzarella) and *fritate* (omelettes).

---

gnocchi in cheese and flavoured with truffles. Good for vegetarians and great for kids, too.

➕ E7 ✉ Piazza Santo Spirito 16r ☎ 055 238 2383 🚍 11, 36, 37, D

RISTORANTE BECCOFINO (€€)

www.beccofino.com
Chic, modern restaurant and wine bar. Experience Tuscan cooking with a twist—the chef worked in New York. In summer there is a terrace over-looking the river. Good wine list.

➕ E6 ✉ Piazza degli Scarlatti 1r ☎ 055 290 076 🚍 6, 11, 36, 37, D

TRATTORIA SANT'AGOSTINO 23 (€€)

www.sa23.it
This new trattoria has a modern twist with brightly coloured art on the walls. Mainly Tuscan cuisine is served although they offer international dishes as well.

➕ D7 ✉ Via Sant'Agostino 23r ☎ 055 210 208 🕐 Closed Mon 🚍 11, 36, 37, D

LE VOLPI E L'UVA (€)

www.levolpieluva.com
A good little wine bar behind the Ponte Vecchio where you can wash down pungent Italian salamis and cheeses with robust Tuscan wines.

➕ F7 ✉ Piazza dei Rossi 1r ☎ 055 239 8132 🕐 Closed Sun 🚍 C, D

There is plenty to do to escape the crowds or to have a change of scenery. Choose from pretty Fiesole, only 7km (4 miles) away; try medieval Siena and Lucca, or the Leaning Tower of Pisa, providing an irresistible pull.

Typical Tuscan country-side (left); Roman amphitheatre (below); the bell tower (right)

Fiesole

Perfectly perched on a hillside 7km (4 miles) above Florence, this delightful Etruscan-Roman town offers outstanding views over the city and the chance to visit an impressive archaeological complex, complete with amphitheatre, baths and a temple.

Take a stroll Fiesole provides the perfect antidote to hectic sightseeing in central Florence, while the bus ride there, climbing the winding road, is a pleasing introduction to the Tuscan countryside. Head first to the tourist information office to pick up a town map, which includes three walking routes that take in the best spots for views.

The archaeological area The entrance ticket to Fiesole's important Roman and Etruscan remains includes the Museo Civico and the small Museo Bandini. Set on a hillside, the open-air site features an Etruscan temple, the superbly preserved first century AD Roman amphitheatre and the partially restored Roman baths. The theatre, holding 3,000 people, is still used today for performances and concerts during the Fiesole Summer Festival (▷ 103). On Via Dupré, Museo Bandini houses 13th- to 15th-century Florentine paintings and Luca della Robbia terracottas.

Around the town Landmarks include the Duomo, with its 13th-century bell tower, and the striking 14th-century Palazzo Communale, now occupied by the town council. Several traditional restaurants and cafes overlook the main square.

THE BASICS

✚ Off map at M1
✉ Via Portigiani 3–5
☎ 055 596 1323
🕐 Mon–Fri 9.30–5.30, Sun and public hols 10–4
🚌 7
♿ Good
🎫 Combined ticket expensive

HIGHLIGHTS

● Views over Florence
● Archaeological area
● Roman amphitheatre
● Walks in the Tuscan countryside

FARTHER AFIELD

TOP 25

TOP 25 *(top left corner)*

More to See

LE CASCINE

Florence's largest park is a long way from the heart of town, badly kept and seedy by night. Long and thin, it was laid out as a public park by Napoleon's sister, Elisa Baciocchi Bonaparte, in 1811, on the site of the Medici dairy pastures (*cascine*). Every Tuesday there is a market, and an open-air swimming pool is also in the park.

➕ A3 ✉ Ponte della Vittoria 🕒 24 hours 🚌 17, 18 ♿ Good 🎫 Free

CERTOSA DI GALLUZZO

This great Carthusian monastery was once occupied by 18 monks, who lived silent lives. The stunning Chiostro Grande is decorated with *tondi* by brothers Andrea and Giovanni della Robbia. The visit includes the Palazzo degli Studi, which holds great *Scenes from the Passion* frescoes, executed by Pontormo while he was sheltered here during the 1522 plague.

➕ Off map at C9 ✉ Certosa di Galluzzo, Via Buca di Certose 2 ☎ 055 204 9226 🕒 Tue– Sat 9.15–11.15, 3–5 🚌 37 ♿ Good 🎫 Free or donation ❓ Guided tours only

FORTEZZA DA BASSO

An enormous defensive fortress built in 1534 by Antonio da Sangallo il Giovane to the orders of Alessandro de' Medici. Today cars and buses hurtle around all sides, while the citadel hosts events and exhibitions.

➕ E3 ✉ Viale Filippo Strozzi ☎ Contact tourist office for events 🚌 4, 12, 13, 14, 20, 23

MUSEO STIBBERT

www.museostibbert.it

This bizarre museum, with superb armour, makes a fascinating diversion. The collection was amassed by Frederick Stibbert, (1838–1906), who travelled the world, purchasing armour porcelain, paintings, costume and much more. The museum is also worth visiting for its wooded grounds, complete with an Egyptian-style folly.

➕ Off map at F1 ✉ Via Frederico Stibbert 26 ☎ 055 475 520/055 486 049 🕒 Mon–Wed 10–2, Fri–Sun 10–6; ticket office closes 1 hour before museum 🚌 4 to Via Vittorio Emanuele II and steep 5-min walk to museum ♿ Most parts have access 🎫 Moderate ❓ Café and bookshop

Il Gioco del Ponte, *painted in the 17th century, is on display in Museo Stibbert*

Excursions

LUCCA

A prosperous town entirely enclosed within superb Renaissance walls with a rich heritage of churches and palaces.

The best starting point is Piazza Napoleone, with all the main sights only a few minutes' walk away. Begin at the Duomo, and its Museo della Cattedrale, then cross the square to Santi Giovanni e Reparata. Via Fillungo is an expensive shopping street that leads north to the Piazza Anfiteatro and San Frediano, another outstanding church. The main museums lie inside the walls to the west and east of the heart of town. Walking around the walls gives a fine overview of the town. The walls, which are 4km (2.5 miles) long, also give a spectacular view of the countryside farther afield; you can even see the distant Apuan Alps, which are covered in snow in winter.

THE BASICS

www.luccaturismo.it
Distance: 50km (31 miles)
Journey Time: About 1 hour
🚆 Regular departures from Santa Maria Novella station to Lucca Centrale
🛈 Piazza Santa Maria 35, Porto San Donato, Pizzzale Verdi
☎ 0583 919 931; 0583 419 689

PISA

The main draw is the stunning architecture of the Campo dei Miracoli (Field of Miracles), home to the famous Leaning Tower.

The tower, reopened in 2001 after years of work to steady the tilt, stands next to the Romanesque-Gothic Duomo and Baptistery, the largest in Italy. All three buildings date from the 11th and 12th centuries, at the height of Pisa's power.

There is, however, more to Pisa than just its tower. The city is home to some 87,500 residents and there are more than 20 churches, several palaces and historic bridges to be explored. The pleasant cobbled streets of the shopping centre are a good place to stroll and find a café or restaurant. Check out the markets and mingle with the locals away from the tourist area around the tower. The daily food market (7–1.30) held in Piazza delle Vettovaglie, just off Borgo Stretto, is particularly lively.

THE BASICS

www.pisaturismo.it
Distance: 80km (50 miles)
Journey Time: 1 hour
🚆 Regular departures from Santa Maria Novella station to Pisa Centrale Station
🛈 Piazza Arcivescovado 8
☎ 050 42291

FARTHER AFIELD

EXCURSIONS

THE BASICS

www.terresiena.it
Distance: 66km (41 miles)
Journey Time: 1–2 hours
Regular departures from Santa Maria Novella station
Rapide Sita bus leaves the Florence bus station to San Domenico in Sienna
Piazza del Campo 56
0577 280 551

SIENA

One of the loveliest towns in Italy, with great museums, interesting shops and many hills.

The focal point is fan-shape Piazza del Campo, which slopes down to the bell tower. The Gothic cathedral was built between 1136 and 1382. Outside is a vast unfinished nave, begun in 1339 with the intention of making this the world's largest cathedral. Work was abandoned during the plague of 1348. Siena is home to the famous Palio, a horse race held in Piazza del Campo on 2 July and 16 August. Tickets for the event sell out months in advance; it is possible to stand but it does get very crowded and can be very hot. For a sense of Siena's size and layout, get a bird's-eye view by climbing the Torre del Mangia or the old cathedral wall. The historic centre of the city is closed to traffic making it easy for pedestrians, and fortunately all the main sights are in close proximity and easily walkable.

THE BASICS

www.sangimignano.it
Distance: 57km (35 miles)
Journey Time: 1 hour
Route: Take the Firenze/ Siena *raccordo* (a motorway link road) until the Poggibonsi exit. Follow the signs from here to San Gimignano–around 6km (4 miles)
Museo Leonardiano
Castello dei Conti Guidi, Vinci
0571 933251
Mar–end Oct daily 9.30–7; Nov–end Feb 9.30–6
Moderate

TUSCAN COUNTRYSIDE

A country drive is a real treat. Much-visited San Gimignano is a prime destination with its hilltop site and medieval towers.

San Gimignano is the archetypical Tuscan town, perched on a hilltop and surrounded by vine-yards, olive groves and cypress trees. The towers of the medieval town can be seen from some distance away. Only 15 of the original 72 towers remain, but their impact is still breathtaking. There are several museums to visit and particular products to buy, including San Gimignano wine and olive oil. For pots, stop in Montelupo, where many of Florence's ceramics have been made for centuries. On your way back visit Vinci, the birthplace of Leonardo da Vinci with a museum about his life. If you want a swim, the village of Sambuca, near Tavarnelle, has an outdoor pool. Deep in the countryside you can find olives and wine for sale.

Lucca

CANIPAROLI

This shop is a choco-holic's heaven. Chunks of chocolate adorn the window, along with calorific but divine cakes, such as the naughty but delicious *sachertorte*.

✉ Via Paolino 96 ☎ 0583 53456 🕒 Tue–Sat 9.30–1, 3.30–7.30

CERAMICHE DI SUGARÒ

www.sugaro.it
The highly decorative traditional ceramics in this shop conjure up the warm tones of the Tuscan countryside. Everything for the table from huge platters to delightful egg cups in the shape of a chicken. Your goods can be shipped home.

✉ Piazza Napoleone 17 ☎ 0583 464 557 🕒 Closed Mon am

CERAMISTI D'ARTÉ

www.ceramistidarte.it
Tuscan artists Stefano Seardo and Fabrizio Falchi sculpt and paint at this workshop. Visit to pick up hand-painted decorative tiles, terracotta sculptures and marble mosaics. Everything is produced according to ancient Italian ceramic techniques.

✉ Via Mordini 74/78 ☎ 0583 492 700 🕒 Tue–Sun 9.30–1, 3.30–8, Mon 3.30–7.30

MARSILI COSTANTINO

Marsali gives a tasty introduction to Lucca's local vineyards, with some lesser-known but delicious wines. Also try some of the herb liqueurs and *digestifs* that are pro-duced using local recipes.

✉ Piazza San Michele 38 ☎ 0583 491 751 🕒 Jun–end Sep daily 9–7.30; Oct–end May Tue–Sat 9–1, 3.30–7.30, Mon 3.30–7.30

TADDEUCCI

www.taddeucci.com
This shop, founded by Jacopo Taddeucci in 1881, is in Lucca's main square. It is renowned for the *buccellato*, a sweet ring-shape cake made with raisins and flavoured with anise. Plenty more cakes and patisserie to choose from, together with sweets and chocolates.

✉ Piazza San Michele 34 ☎ 0583 494 933 🕒 Daily 8.30–8 (closed Thu Nov–Feb)

HANDICRAFTS

Tuscany has a strong artisan tradition that continues to flourish. There is a huge range of regional handicrafts to seek out, such as olive-wood bowls and plates, alabaster ware and glass-ware, with many products only available in the area where they are made. Florence and the surround-ing area has an abundance of small craft workshops specializing in picture frames, accessories and restored antique furniture.

Pisa

BACCHUS ENOTECA

www.bacchusenoteca.com
Just a short distance from the main train station, this specialist wine shop is the perfect place to buy the best of Tuscan wines. You will also find spirits and liqueurs, as well as sweets, oils and other delicacies.

✉ Via Mascagni 1 ☎ 050 500 560 🕒 Tue–Sun 9–1, 4–8

FEDERICO SALZA

This Pisan outlet of a popular Turin confectioner sells beautiful fashioned chocolates and pastry goods. Look for the chocolate Leaning Tower of Pisa.

✉ Borgo Stretto 46 ☎ 050 580 244 🕒 Jun–end Oct daily 8–8.30; Nov–end May Tue–Sun 8–8.30

LENZI GHINO GIACOMO

This factory shop, to the west of Pisa toward Vicopisano, sells classic Tuscan ceramics and it's owners pride themselves on producing basins, vases and pottery the traditional way. Choose from vases and crockery splashed with green and white—they are beautifully decorated pots for storing oil, wine and herbs, and make great gifts.

✉ Via Provinciale Vicarese 371, San Giovanni alla Vena ☎ 050 799 015 🕒 Mon–Sat 9–1, 3–8

Siena

ANTICHITÀ MONNA AGNESE

One of Siena's better antiques stores, stocking furniture and silver amid other items. There is another, smaller shop on the opposite side of the street, which deals in antique jewellery.
✉ Via di Città 45 and 60
☎ 0577 282 288

CERAMICHE ARTISHICHE SANTA CATERINA

A family business run by the founder, Marcello Neri, his wife and son. The whole family works in the traditional Sienese styles of ceramics using only black, white and *terra di Siena,* or burnt siena glass glazes. Their designs are inspired by local architecture, especially the Duomo, and you can watch them at work.
✉ Via di Città 74 ☎ 0577 283 098

CORTECCI ABBIGLIAMENTO

In business since 1935, this shop's large collection of men's and women's designer labels includes Gucci, Armani, Yves Saint Laurent, Christian Dior, Roberto Cavalli and Dolce & Gabbana. There are two branches of this shop and this one has the more classic collections, while the other branch at Il Campo 30, stocks labels aimed at a younger market.
✉ Via Banchi di Sopra 27
☎ 0577 280 096

DROGHERIA MANGANELLI

A must for foodies. It is a member of the Slow Food Movement, an organization that promotes organic food, grown and cooked using a traditional method. Drogheria Manganelli has been selling local produce since 1879, including cured meats, fine farmhouse cheeses, vinegars, wine, the best virgin olive oils and *ricciarelli* (almond cookies). Traditionally served with sweet wine, these cookies are enjoyed year-round.

MARKETS

There are daily food markets in provincial and regional capitals and other large towns. They generally take place in a purpose-built market hall or in a specific square or street, selling meat, groceries, fish, dairy products, fruit and vegetables. Where there's a daily food market, the weekly market will be devoted to everything else from clothes and shoes to household goods, plants and fabrics. In Florence the most prominent are Mercato Centrale (▷ 68), Mercato di Sant'Ambrogio (▷ 38) and Mercato Nuovo (▷ 37).

✉ Via di Città 71–73
☎ 0577 280 002

MORBIDI

One of the best-known Sienese delicatessens, selling Tuscan salamis and the more unusual *finochiona* (salami made from fennel). Be sure to try the local cheeses, such as *pecorino* or the oval-shaped *fresco di Monnalisa*, and pâtés that are great for picnics.
✉ Via Banchi di Sopra 75
☎ 0577 280 268

SIENA RICAMA

This embroidery and needlework shop is run by Signora Fontani, who makes all the goods himself. Drawing inspiration from medieval designs, local art, frescoes and manuscripts, the embroidered or cross-stitched items include clothing, soft furnishings, lampshades and tapestries.
✉ Via di Città 61 ☎ 0577 288 339

TESSUTI A MANO

Drop into this workshop and boutique to pick up beautiful, hand-woven accessories and fashionable garments. Designer Fioretta Bacci can often be seen sitting at a loom weaving her much sought-after scarves, shawls and items of clothing.
✉ Via San Pietro 7
☎ 0577 282 200

Entertainment and Nightlife

AUDITORIUM FLOG
www.flog.it
This is probably the best known of Florence's live music venues, where music of all kinds is played; regular themed disco evenings.
🔲 Off map 📧 Via Mercati 24b ☎ 055 487 145 🚌 4

CENTRAL PARK
At this complex, with garden, eight bars, four dance floors, restaurant and VIP terrace, Italian house dominates but there's also plenty of room for loungecore and smooth piano-bar music.
🔲 B4 📧 Via del Fosso Macinate 2, Parco delle Cascine ☎ 055 353 505 🕐 Closed Mon 🚌 1, 9, 12, 80

ESTATE FIESOLANA
A season of music, opera and ballet known as the Sunset Concerts, primarily in Fiesole's open-air Teatro Romano (▷ 97), from late June to September. Reserve in advance and then head for the Fiesole hills, above the city. The concerts are an unbeatable experience.
Estate Fiesolana
🔲 Off map ☎ Contact APT (tourist information), Fiesole 055 596 1323
Teatro Romano
🔲 Off map 📧 Via Marini 🚌 7

GIRASOL
www.girasol.it
Florentines have a passion for Latin American

bars. This is the best, with live and recorded Cuban, Caribbean and other Latin-American music.
🔲 D1 📧 Via del Romito 1r ☎ 055 474 948 🚌 14

PALASPORT
This medium-size venue near Campo Marte hosts some of Italy's most celebrated rock and pop acts like Pino Daniele and Ligabue. Check in advance for British and US bands who may be swinging into Palasport.
🔲 M4 📧 Viale P Paoli 3 ☎ Box office Via Alamanini 055 210 804 for tickets 🚌 3, 10

PALAZZO DEI CONGRESSI
This palazzo hosts many conferences and cultural events throughout the year. Look out for the occasional choral and classical concerts held in one of the fine salons.

🔲 E3 📧 Viale Filippo Strozzi ☎ Box office Via Alamanini 055 210 804 for tickets; check with tourist office for events 🚌 6, 11, 22, 36, 37, A

PINOCCHIO JAZZ
Some of Italy's top jazz artists can be heard during the two-season agenda. Members nod approvingly in this smoky venue while the enthusiastic musicians play into the night. Check *Firenze Spettacolo* for what's on.
🔲 M8 📧 Viale Giannotti 13 ☎ 055 683 388 🚌 31, 32

MECCANO
This large, popular and hip club caters for a wide range of tastes including mainstream, house and funk, primarily aimed at a young crowd. It's like one big house party on several floors and a chance to let your hair down after all that culture.
🔲 B4 📧 Via degli Olmi, Parco delle Cascine ☎ 055 331 371 🕐 Closed Mon, Sun 🚌 1, 9, 27,80

TENAX
Trendy and up-to-date music and a huge dance floor; very popular with both Florentines and foreigners. As a superclub, it has some mind-blowing lighting and sound technology and some very curious art installations. Also hosts various live music acts.
🔲 Off map 📧 Via Pratese 46 ☎ 055 308 160 🕐 Check schedule 🚌 29, 30

FARTHER AFIELD

ENTERTAINMENT AND NIGHTLIFE

Sport

CANOTTIERI COMUNALI FIRENZE

Have a go at boating, rowing or canoeing at this club on the River Arno. Courses are available.

🔲 L7 ✉ Lungarno Ferrucci 2 ☎ 055 681 2151 🚌 3, 8, 31, 32, 80

CIRCOLO DEL GOLF DELL'UGOLINO

www.golfugolino.it

Founded in 1933 and designed by British architects, this 18-hole, 72-par attractive course has hosted many famous golfing greats.

🔲 Off map to south ✉ Via Chiantigiana 3, Grassina (10km/6miles south on road to Siena) ☎ 055 230 1009

CLUB SPORTIVO FIRENZE TENNIS

Situated in the park, Le Cascine, just to the west of central Florence; there are two clay courts (covered in winter) in pleasant surroundings.

🔲 A4 ✉ Viale del Visarno 10 ☎ 055 332 701 🚌 1, 9, 12, 16, 26, 27, 80

GOLF CLUB MONTELUPO

www.golfmontelupo.it

This 3,067 yard, par 36, 9-hole golf course lies below the Chianti Montalbano hills on the banks of the Arno. Enjoy the scenery and excellent facilities, including a pro shop, practice area and putting greens. Coaching is available.

🔲 Off map ✉ Fattoria di Fibbiana, Via le Piagge 4, Montelupo (19km/12 miles to west of Florence) ☎ 0571 541 004 🕐 Call for times

IPPODROME FIORENTINI

The Ippodromo delle Mulina is the place to go and see horse racing in Florence where you will find flat racing or trotting racing. Telephone or check the local press for meetings. The track also stages polo events.

🔲 B4 ✉ Le Cascine ☎ 055 422 591; trotting 055 422 59217 🚌 14

PAGANELLI

Open six days a week for swimming, there are also courses for adults and children, which include diving and aquagym.

FOOTBALL IS ALL

Many Florentines take more pride in their football (soccer) team than in their artistic heritage. Until 2002 AC Fiorentina, also known as the 'Viola' (the Purples), were one of the top clubs in Italy, but following a financial scandal the club was declared bankrupt and demoted three divisions. The team clawed its way back into Serie A and regained its former glory. Games take place at the Stadio Artemio Franchi, where you can join the ever-faithful fans cheering on the lads in lavender.

🔲 Off map ✉ Viale Guidoni 208, Novoli ☎ 055 437 9787 🕐 Closed Tue 🚌 5, 22

PALESTRA TROPOS

www.troposfirenze.it

This well-established gym has classes for all ages, including aerobics and hydrobike exercises. Two swimming pools.

🔲 K6 ✉ Via Orcagna 20a ☎ 055 659 746 🚌 14, 31, 32

PISCINA COMUNALE BELLARIVA

An outdoor Olympic swimming pool with a smaller one for children in pleasant shady gardens east of the city.

🔲 M7 ✉ Lungarno A Moro ☎ 055 677 521 🕐 Jun–Sep 🚌 14

PISCINA LE PAVONIERE

Most popular and the prettiest outdoor swimming pool in Florence, in Le Cascine (▷ 98).

🔲 A4 ✉ Viale della Catena 2 ☎ 055 321 5644 🕐 Jun–Sep 🚌 17

STADIO COMUNALE ARTEMIO FRANCHI

The Stadio Comunale Artemio Franchi or the Palazzo dello Sport, is where AC Fiorentina (▷ panel) play football (soccer). Games take place on alternate Sundays from September to May. Tickets are available at the entrance and in cafés near by.

🔲 L3 ✉ Campo di Marte, Viale Manfredo Fanti 4 🚌 17

Restaurants

PRICES

Prices are approximate, based on a 3-course meal for one person.

€€€	over €45
€€	€20–€45
€	under €20

Fiesole

RISTORANTE IL FIESOLANO (PERSEUS) (€€)

This is one of Florence's best restaurants in which to sample the famous *bistecca alla fiorentina* (▷ panel). Other classic Tuscan dishes are served on a terrace facing the Teatro Romano in Fiesole.
🚫 Off map at M1 ⊠ Piazza Mino da Fiesole 9 ☎ 055 591 43 🕐 Limited winter opening 🚌 7

RISTORANTE I POLPA (€€)

Eat at this friendly place and enjoy a magnificent night view over Florence. Not only is there an open wood-burning grill, but the oven is lighted, too, for cooking *crostini*—toasted crusty bread with a variety of toppings.
🚫 Off map at M1 ⊠ Piazza Mino da Fiesole 21–22 ☎ 055 50485 🕐 Thu–Tue 7–10 🚌 7

RISTORANTE SAN MICHELE (€€€)

The evocative former monastery setting and some of the finest cuisine in the area attract diners to this Fiesole restaurant in the hotel Villa San Michele (▷ 112).
🚫 Off map at M1 ⊠ Via Doccia 4 ☎ 055 567 8200 🕐 Daily lunch and dinner; closed end-Nov to end-Mar 🚌 7

Lucca

BUCA DI SANT ANTONIO (€€)

www.bucadisantantonio.com
One of the oldest, as well as the most popular, restaurants in Lucca. The menu is all à la carte, with an emphasis on Lucchese cuisine, and the use of seasonal, freshly produced ingredients.
⊠ Via della Cervia 3 ☎ 0583 55881 🕐 Tue–Sat lunch and dinner, Sun lunch

OSTERIA MACHIAVELLI (€–€€)

Small trattoria a few

> **NATURALLY ROBUST**
>
> The classic Florentine dish is *bistecca alla fiorentina* (T-bone steak sold by the weight, usually 100g). Grilled and served rare with lemon, it can be found in the majority of Florentine restaurants. Other traditional dishes include *trippa alla fiorentina* (tripe stewed with tomatoes and served with Parmesan), *crostini* (toasted bread and a pâté of roughly chopped chicken livers), and *panzanella* (a salad of crumbled bread tossed with tomatoes with olive oil, onions, basil and parsley).

paces from Piazza San Salvatore in the middle of Lucca. Predominantly Tuscan and Lucchese cuisine with the usual mixture of cold cuts, a range of interesting sausages, grilled meats, roasts and home-made pastas. Try the salted cod with leeks or the tasty grilled pork ribs. Small but well-chosen wine list to complement your meal.
⊠ Via C Battisti 28 ☎ 0583 467 219 🕐 Mon–Sat lunch and dinner

ROUSSEAU IL DOGANIERE (€–€€)

www.rousseauildoganiere.it
Full of character, this restaurant and pizzeria serves good fresh home-made pasta, beef dishes sourced from local cattle, fish, soup and excellent pizza from the traditional firewood oven. Outdoor seating in summer.
⊠ Via Vittorio Emanuele II 28 ☎ 0583 584 214 🕐 Wed–Mon lunch and dinner

TRATTORIA DA LEO (€)

www.trattoriadaleo.it
Popular family-run trattoria where you can eat in the dining room, with its pastel walls and wooden furnishings, or on the simple but shaded terrace. The owners make you feel at home, sometimes sitting and chatting after the meal.
⊠ Via Tegrimi 1 ☎ 0583 492 236 🕐 Daily lunch and dinner

FARTHER AFIELD

RESTAURANTS

Pisa

LA BUCA (€–€€)
www.labuca.org
In a popular spot in the heart of Pisa, Buca draws the crowds to its pleasant terrace and the set-price lunch menu, which offers Tuscan cuisine at a reasonable price. Dinner is little more formal but still with lots of pizza and pasta choices.
✉ Via G Tassi 6/B ☎ 050 560 660 🕓 Sat–Thu lunch and dinner

DE BRUNO (€€–€€€)
www.anticatrattoriadabruno.com
Self-proclaimed as the best restaurant in Pisa, this long-established trattoria serves traditional local cuisine. The two dining rooms have wood-beamed ceilings, long, elegant tables, and white-washed walls covered with photographs of the famous people who have dined here under patron Piero Cei's watchful eye. Reserve in advance.
✉ Via Luigi Bianchi 12 ☎ 050 560 818 🕓 Wed–Sun lunch and dinner

Siena

AL MARSILI (€€–€€€)
www.ristorantealmarsili.it
Not far from the cathedral, this is one of Siena's classiest restaurants where you can try Sienese cuisine in an attractive vaulted dining room. The menu includes both traditional dishes and some more creative takes on the local cuisine. Sample one of their most famous dishes, the *faraona alla Medici* (meaty guinea fowl cooked with pine nuts, almonds and prunes) or the tasty lemon risotto.
✉ Via del Castoro 3 ☎ 0577 47154 🕓 Tue–Sun lunch and dinner

IL CAMPO (€–€€)
This is the original restaurant on the Piazza del Campo and a great spot for people-watching. A consequence of this is that service may suffer at busy times. The menu is a mix of Italian and European cusine. They don't take reservations.
✉ Piazza del Campo 50–51 ☎ 0577 280 725

ICE CREAM

Italian ice cream–*gelato*–is generally of very high quality. Italians would rather pay more and eat something made with fresh ingredients. So a basic ice cream is usually made with milk, cream, eggs and sugar, and the tastes are strikingly pure and direct. A popular choice is *crema*–egg custard–good with a scoop of intense dark chocolate or pungent coffee. People usually opt for a selection of *creme* or *frutte* (creams or fruit) and don't mix the two types. The best *gelaterie* serve fruit varieties made from whatever fruits are in season.

🕓 Wed–Mon lunch and dinner

OSTERIA LE LOGGE (€€–€€€)
www.giannibrunelli.it
In a former medieval pharmacy, this charming restaurant is just off the Campo. There are tables outside, plus two dining areas. The menu is full of classic Tuscan dishes. Reservations are advised.
✉ Via del Porrione 33 ☎ 0577 48013 🕓 Mon–Sat lunch and dinner

SOTTO LE FONTI (€€)
www.sottolefonti.it
This medieval building has been beautifully renovated to recreate an old-fashioned restaurant. The menu is based on Sienese dishes, such as salami, game, or lamb chops with juniper. The scrumptious cakes and desserts are all home-made.
✉ Via Esterna Fonteblanda 14 ☎ 0577 226 446 🕓 Daily lunch and dinner

LA TAVERNA DI SAN GIUSEPPE (€–€€)
A lively group of young people run this trattoria. It specializes in Tuscan food, with an emphasis on meat, although vegetarians are well catered to with a rich vegetable soup, *ribollita*. Intimate cellar-like dining room.
✉ Via Giovanni Duprè 132 ☎ 0577 42286 🕓 Mon–Sat lunch and dinner; closed last 2 weeks in Jan and Jul

Florence is one of Italy's top destinations and hotels are, on the whole, expensive. Check out the Internet before leaving home to catch some seasonal deals. Staying out of season is your best bet.

Introduction

Choose from world-class hotels in historic buildings, ultrachic boutique hotels or family-run *pensiones* that haven't changed much in 30 years. Houses and apartments offering bed and breakfast are an option that is becoming very popular.

Hotels

Tuscan hotels (*alberghi*) are graded by the regional authorities on a star rating of one to five. These refer to the facilities provided rather than character or comfort. Expect five-star hotels to be grand, with superb facilities and service; four-star establishments will be almost as good. Three-star hotels are more idiosyncratic. Prices can vary enormously, as can the public areas and staffing levels; but all rooms will have a television and telephone. One and two stars are relatively inexpensive, clean and comfortable, and rooms almost always have private bathrooms in two-star places. Breakfast is usually included, although often poor.

Pensiones

There's little difference between simpler hotels and *pensiones*; both are usually family-run, and provide spotlessly clean, comfortable rooms at a fair price. Some *pensiones* may be a little dated, but this is also the case in smaller hotels.

Rooms to Rent

Signs saying rooms (*camere* or *zimmer*) are rooms to rent in private houses and are a good option if money is tight or you can't find a hotel. Local tourist offices keep a list.

RESERVATIONS

Florence is so popular that you will need to book in advance at whatever time of year you decide to visit. If you're booking in advance from home, make certain you get written confirmation and take it with you. Without this, you may turn up and find all knowledge of your booking denied. If you make an internet booking, print out your booking confirmation and take it with you.

You will appreciate somewhere comfortable to relax and unwind after your journey or a day sightseeing

Budget Hotels

WHERE TO STAY BUDGET HOTELS

PRICES

Expect to pay up to €100 for a double room in a budget hotel

ALBERGO FIRENZE
www.hotelfirenze-fi.it
A 57-room modern hotel in a very quiet courtyard in the heart of Florence.
⊞ F6 ✉ Piazza dei Donati 4 ☎ 055 214 203 🚍 A

BRETAGNA
www.hotelbretagna.net
Eighteen affordable rooms with views of the River Arno.
⊞ E6 ✉ Lungarno Corsini 6 ☎ 055 289 618 619 🚍 B

CHIAZZA
www.chiazzahotel.com
In the Santa Croce area, this hotel has been refurbished and offers a smart, comfortable budget option. Not far from the Duomo, some of the 14 rooms look out onto the terracotta-tiled rooftops.
⊞ H5 ✉ Borgo Piniti 5 ☎ 055 248 0363 🚍 14, 23, A

CRISTINA
www.hotelcristina-florence.com
A small, friendly hotel in a medieval palace off a quiet street in the heart of Florence. The nine rooms (four ensuite) have high ceilings and wood furniture. It's good value and the delightful owners make it perfect for families. Because of this it is a popular choice so make reservations well ahead.

⊞ F6 ✉ Via della Condotta 4 ☎ 055 214 484 🚍 A

JOHANNA I
www.johanna.it
Beautifully renovated, the 11 rooms are small but beautifully furnished and there is an intimate communal room with a fridge.
⊞ G3 ✉ Via Bonifacio Lupi 14 ☎ 055 481 896 🚍 8, 12, 20

NUOVA ITALIA
www.hotel-nuovaitalia.com
Modern, clean 20-room hotel with friendly staff.
⊞ E4 ✉ Via Faenza 26 ☎ 055 287 508 🚍 12

PENSIONE MARIA LUISA DE' MEDICI
Characterful 17th-century house cluttered with objects d'art. The nine rooms vary in size—some very large and two with private bathroom. Excellent value with breakfast included, and

CAMPING

Campeggio Michelangelo is on the hills south of the Arno yet is only a short bus ride to central Florence. It has hot showers, clean toilets, washing machines, electricity points, internet access, a supermarket and a bar with a terrace that looks out over the city. There are 240 pitches. Open all year
⊞ H8 ✉ Via Michelangelo 80 ☎ 055 681 1977; www.camping.it 🚍 12, 13

very close to the Duomo. Not for night owls as the owner has a curfew (time varies with season).
⊞ F5 ✉ Via del Corso 1 ☎ 055 280 048 🚍 14, 23, A

SCOTI
www.hotelscoti.com
Atmospheric 15th-century building in an excellent location directly opposite the Palazzo Strozzi in the shopping mecca of Via de' Tornabuoni. It's a great place to stay—excellent value, with period character, and a good central base from which to explore the city. The 11 bedrooms are simple and light. There are no private bathrooms, but the shared ones are very clean. The lounge area has attractive 18th-century frescoes depicting Italian landscapes.
⊞ E6 ✉ Via de' Tornabuoni 7 ☎ 055 292 128 🚍 6, 11, 36, A

SORELLE BANDINI
Perfect for the more bohemian visitor, this slightly ramshackle *pensione* is on the top floor of a 1505 palazzo and has a fabulous loggia that is ideal for picnics, and 13 huge rooms (five with bathroom) with frescoed, slightly crumbling ceilings. The breakfast room looks over a panorama of terracotta tile roofs to the Palazzo Pitti.
⊞ E7 ✉ Piazza Santo Spirito 9 ☎ 055 215 308 🚍 36, 37, D

Mid-Range Hotels

PRICES

Expect to pay between €100 and €200 for a double room in a mid-range hotel

ANNALENA

www.hotelannalena.it
In a Medici palazzo opposite the Boboli Gardens, this hotel was once the haunt of artists and writers. Some of the 20 rooms have terraces and views. A lovely peaceful spot.
🏠 D8 ✉ Via Romana 34
☎ 055 222 402 🚌 11, 36, 37, D

BALESTRI

www.hotel-balestri.it
Close to the River Arno, between the Uffizi and Santa Croce, with 51 comfortable rooms.
🏠 F5 ✉ Piazza Mentana 7
☎ 055 214 743 🚌 23, B

BELLETTINI

www.hotelbellettini.com
Close to San Lorenzo and the Duomo, this hotel, with 28 rooms and 5 suites, dates from the 15th century, making it one of the oldest in Florence as well as one of the friendliest. Rooms come in a variety of sizes; optional private bathroom. Breakfast includes owner's home baking and should not be missed.
🏠 F5 ✉ Via de'Conti 7
☎ 055 213 561 🚌 1, 6, 7, 10, 11, 14, 17

CASCI

www.hotelcasci.com
A family-run hotel, with 25 rooms, and once home to the Italian composer Gioacchino Rossini. Although modernized, it still has some of its original 14th-century features. Immaculate, functional rooms a short stroll from the Duomo.
🏠 F4 ✉ Via Cavour 13
☎ 055 211 686 🚌 1, 6, 7, 10, 11, 17

LE DUE FONTANE

www.leduefontane.it
Modern 57-room hotel in the delightful Piazza della Santissima Annunziata.
🏠 G4 ✉ Piazza della Santissima Annunziata 14
☎ 055 210 185 🚌 6, 31, 32, C

GALILEO

www.galileohotel.it
Bright and cheerful hotel ideal for those who want to make the most of every minute in Florence. The 31 rooms are clean

WHICH ROOM?

The room with a view is a much sought-after thing. However, it can often come with street noise. Most Florentini hotels are in palazzi built around courtyards, so the rooms with views face onto the street, while the ones looking over the courtyards are pleasantly quiet. You might prefer to forego the romance to ensure a good night's sleep.

and relaxing and have all the amenities you might require.
🏠 E4 ✉ Via Nazionale 22a
☎ 055 496 645 🚌 4, 12, 25, 31, 32

HERMITAGE

www.hermitagehotel.com
A well-known 29-room hotel overlooking the Ponte Vecchio, which draws visitors back time and time again. Idyllic, light and airy roof garden.
🏠 F6 ✉ Vicolo Marzio 1, Piazza del Pesce ☎ 055 287 216 🚌 B

KRAFT

www.krafthotel.it
This hotel has been renovated to include energy-saving technology in the 80 comfortable rooms. There is a small rooftop swimming pool and some terrific views.
🏠 C5 ✉ Via Solferino 2
☎ 055 284 273 🚌 B, D

LOGGIATO DEI SERVITI

www.loggiatodeiservitihotel.it
You can relax under vaulted ceilings, amid dark-wood antiques and rich fabrics in the former monastery of the Serviti. The rooms are enlivened by bright curtains and throws. Many look onto the arcades of Piazza Santissima Annunziate. The 38 rooms have private bathrooms and the breakfast room has views of the Accademia gardens.
🏠 G4 ✉ Piazza Santissima Annunziata 3 ☎ 055 289 592
🚌 6, 31, 32, C

MARIO'S
www.hotelmarios.com
This small family-run hotel is an example of the great value for money that can still be found in this expensive city. It feels as if you are staying in someone's home, with care and attention paid to the 16 atmospheric rooms and to your needs.
🔲 E4 ✉ Via Faenza 89 ☎ 055 216 801 🚌 4, 7, 10, 12, 13, 25, 31, 32, 33

PALAZZO RUSPOLI
www.palazzo-ruspoli.it
Ideally placed close to the Duomo and San Lorenzo, this 20-room hotel is an immaculate and comfortable place to stay with its attractive paintwork and patterned soft furnishings.
🔲 F5 ✉ Via de' Martelli 5 ☎ 055 267 05635 🚌 1, 6, 7, 11, 17

LA RESIDENZA
www.laresidenzahotel.com
Comfortable 23-room hotel on the top four floors of a 17th-century palazzo on the super-elegant Via de' Tornabuoni. A complete overhaul has resulted in some exceptionally well-appointed rooms with huge bathrooms. Rooms at the top have balconies and there is a small roof terrace. Friendly and considerate owners ensure an enjoyable stay. Free internet access is available.
🔲 E6 ✉ Via de' Tornabuoni 8 ☎ 055 218 684 🚌 6, 11, 36, 37, A

RIVOLI
www.hotelrivoli.it
Close to Santa Maria Novella, the Rivoli is a beautifully renovated Franciscan monastery. The 80 rooms are well furnished with large marble bathrooms and some have a balcony or terrace.
🔲 E5 ✉ Via della Scala 33 ☎ 055 278 61 🚌 11, 36, 37, A

LA SCALETTA
www.lascaletta.com
For those who want to stay on the quieter south side of the River Arno, La Scaletta is in a peaceful spot close to Oltrarno and the Boboli Gardens. The 14 rooms have a homey feel. Lovely rooftop terrace.
🔲 E7 ✉ Via de Guicciardini 13 ☎ 055 283 028 🚌 D

PRICING
Italian hotels are legally required to post rates for high and low season on the back of every bedroom door. You should agree on a price before making a reservation. Rates vary according to the season, sometimes by as much as 25 per cent. Some hotels charge the same rate year-round. Hotels often quote their most expensive rates. So if you want a particular hotel ask if they have a less expensive room.

TORNABUONI BEACCI
www.tornabuonihotels.com
Handsome hotel that's great for shopping and sightseeing. The large, leafy roof garden and antiques-filled lounge are quiet retreats from the bustle outside on this busy street. The 28 bedrooms are simple and uncluttered, and each has its own private bathroom.
🔲 E6 ✉ Via de' Tornabuoni 3 ☎ 055 212 645 🚌 6, 11, 36, 37, A

VILLA FIESOLE
www.villafiesole.it
In the hilltop village of Fiesole, this hotel with 32 rooms, has an outdoor pool and a wonderful Victorian greenhouse that accommodates the breakfast room, a lounge area and several bedoooms. This hotel offers really good value for great surroundings.
🔲 Off map at M1 ✉ Via Beato Angelico 35 ☎ 055 597 252 🚌 7

VILLANI
www.hotelvillani.it
Experience real value for the money at this 13-roomed hotel that attracts an interesting array of visitors, including Italian families. It's situated conveniently close to the Duomo. There are great views from the top floor terrace.
🔲 F5 ✉ Via delle Oche 11 ☎ 055 239 6451 🚌 A

Luxury Hotels

BRUNELLESCHI

www.hotelbrunelleschi.it

A modern 96-room hotel housed in a medieval tower in a peaceful location just behind the Via Calzaiuoli.

⊕ F5 ⊠ Piazza Santa Elisabetta 3 ☎ 055 27370 🚌 A

GRAND HOTEL

http://grandhotel.hotelinfirenze.com

Sumptuous hotel in a 19th-century palazzo overlooking the River Arno. 107 gorgeously decorated rooms.

⊕ D5 ⊠ Piazza Ognissanti 1 ☎ 055 288 781 🚌 A, B

GRAND HOTEL VILLA MEDICI

www.villamedicihotel.com

A little way from the main attractions, this hotel is peaceful and has lovely gardens and a pool overlooked by the top-notch restaurant. Elegant public rooms, classy bedrooms and a fitness centre complete the picture.

⊕ D4 ⊠ Via Il Prato 42 ☎ 055 277 171 🚌 B, D

HELVETIA & BRISTOL

www.royaldemeure.com

An 18th-century hotel in a superb location near the Duomo. Each of the 34 rooms and 18 suites is decorated individually with rich furnishings, and some have antiques, too.

⊕ E5 ⊠ Via dei Pescioni 2 ☎ 055 266 51 🚌 6, 11, 36, 37, A

J. K. PLACE

www.jkplace.com

This small, chic hotel is a fabulous blend of old and new, where modern art is cleverly displayed alongside antique features. Oozing sophistication, the sleek bedrooms and homey day rooms are portrayed with attention to detail. There's a pleasant rooftop terrace.

⊕ E5 ⊠ Piazza Santa Maria Novella 7 ☎ 055 264 5181 🚌 All buses to Santa Maria Novella station

PALAZZO MAGNANI FERONI

www.florencepalace.it

This is a grand place to stay by the side of the River Arno. It has an inner courtyard, vaulted ceilings and lots of marble. There are 12 suites in all.

⊕ D6 ⊠ Borgo San Frediano 5 ☎ 055 239 9544 🚌 B, D

RIVA LOFTS FLORENCE

www.rivahotel.it

Superb hotel created from a former factory. Designed by architect Claudio Nardi, the eight fabulous studios offer park or river views. It takes about 30 minutes to walk to central Florence.

⊕ Off map at A4 ⊠ Via Baccio Bandinelli 98 ☎ 055 713 0272 🚌 No buses

SAVOY

www.hotelsavoy.it

This 19th-century building in Piazza Della Republicca is one of Florence's top boutique hotels. 88 sleek rooms and 14 suites.

⊕ F5 ⊠ Piazza della Republicca 7 ☎ 055 27351 🚌 A

VILLA SAN MICHELE

www.villasanmichele.orient-express.com

Nestling in the Fiesole hills high above Florence this former monastery with 46 rooms offers the lushest of surroundings and the plushest of interiors and superb views.

⊕ Off map at M1 ⊠ Via Doccia 4, Fiesole ☎ 055 567 8200 🚌 7

WESTIN EXCELSIOR

www.westinflorence.com

One of the grandest hotels in Florence, renowned for its opulence. Some of the 171 rooms have river views, and there is a roof terrace.

⊕ D5 ⊠ Piazza Ognissanti 3 ☎ 055 271 51 🚌 A, B

Florence is compact and the public transportation good. Walking is probably one of the best and most rewarding ways of getting around. Petty crime is common but the city is relatively safe.

Planning Ahead

When to Go

Florence's peak season runs from March to October, although many consider it virtually uninterrupted. The city is overrun with tour groups in June and July. If you like heat, go in August—although many Florentines are on holiday and some restaurants close, it's a good time to go because everything is quieter.

TIME
Italy is one hour ahead of London, six hours ahead of New York and nine hours ahead of Los Angeles.

AVERAGE DAILY MAXIMUM TEMPERATURES

JAN	FEB	MAR	APR	MAY	JUN	JUL	AUG	SEP	OCT	NOV	DEC
50°F	52°F	59°F	64°F	73°F	79°F	84°F	82°F	79°F	70°F	57°F	54°F
10°C	11°C	15°C	18°C	23°C	26°C	29°C	28°C	26°C	21°C	14°C	12°C

Spring (March to May) is a good time to visit if you want to avoid the summer heat.
Summer (June to August) can be extremely hot and humid, sometimes uncomfortably so in July and August.
Autumn (September to November) is generally the wettest time in Tuscany, and thunderstorms are common in September.
Winter (December to February) temperatures are often similar to those in northern European countries, and rainfall can be high.

WHAT'S ON

January *Pitti Immagine:* Fashion shows at the Fortezza da Basso.
February *Carnevale:* A low-key version of Venice's annual extravaganza.
March *Festa dell'Annunziata* (25 Mar): Traditionally the Florentine new year, with a fair to celebrate in Piazza Santissima Annunziata.
Scoppio del Carro: The Easter Sunday service at the Duomo culminates in an exploding carriage full of fireworks.
April *Mostra Mercato Internazionale dell' Artigianato:* An international

arts and crafts festival in the Fortezza da Basso.
May *Maggio Musicale:* Florence's international music and dance festival.
Festa del Grillo (Sun after Ascension): Crickets are sold in cages, then released in the park of Le Cascine (▷ 98).
June *Calcio in Costume:* An elaborate soccer game between town districts played in medieval costume in Piazza Santa Croce (▷ 33); preceded by a procession.
Festa di San Giovanni (24 Jun): Fireworks are set off in Piazzale Michelangelo

to celebrate the feast of the patron saint of Florence.
Estate Fiesolana (mid-Jun to Sep): A Fiesole arts festival.
September *Festa del Rificolona* (7 Sep): Children carry paper lanterns in Piazza Santissima Annunziata to honour the birth of the Virgin.
October *Amici della Musica* (Oct–Apr): Concerts. Tickets from Teatro della Pergola (☎ 055 226 4316).
November *Festival dei Popoli* (Nov–Dec): A film festival in the Odeon Cinehall (▷ 46), showing international films.

Useful Websites

www.enit.it
Florence is particularly well covered on the Italian Tourist Board website, with information on history, culture, events, accommodation and gastronomy, in several languages.

www.turismo.toscana.it
This site is run by the Tuscan Regional Tourist Board and covers the whole region as well as Florence, the capital.

www.comune.fi.it
Florence City Council site has good information in English. Its tourism, museum and art pages are always up-to-date, with some good links.

www.firenzeturismo.it
The official APT tourism site with plenty of useful information in English.

www.firenze.net
This Florence-based site, in Italian and English, has information on where to go and what to do, with good maps and plenty of links.

www.emmeti.it
Another Italy-based site, in Italian and English, with a good range of information and links for Florence. It is strong on local events and has an online hotel reservation service.

www.initaly.com
This lively US site is clearly run by passionate Italophiles and has excellent planning tips and sightseeing hints.

www.promhotels.it
Useful online hotel booking site for Florence and other Italian destinations.

www.florenceart.it
You can prereserve a timed entrance ticket, to avoid a long wait to the main Florentine museums including the Uffizi via this efficient site.

PRIME TRAVEL SITES

www.fodors.com
A complete travel-planning site. You can research prices and weather; book air tickets, cars and rooms; ask questions (and get answers) from fellow travellers; and find links to other sites.

www.trenitalia.com
The official site of the Italian State Railways.

www.weatheronline.co.uk/Italy.htm
Good three-day weather predictions.

INTERNET ACCESS

Florence is rapidly coming into the 21st-century with its online facilities. WiFi points can be found at the airport, Santa Maria Novella station, many hotels and specialized internet cafes including:

Internet Train
www.internettrain.it
✚ G5 ✉ Via dell'Oriuolo 40r ☎ 055 263 8968
🕐 Mon–Sat 10–10, Fri, Sun 3–9
✚ F6 ✉ Via Porta Rossa 38 ☎ 055 274 1037 🕐 Mon–Sat 9.30am–midnight, Sun 10am–midnight
✚ F4 ✉ Via Guelfa 54–56 ☎ 055 212 204 🕐 Mon–Fri 9–8, Sat–Sun 11–10

More branches in the city.

Getting There

DIRECT FLIGHTS

There are no direct intercontinental flights to Florence so visitors have to fly to Milan (298km/185 miles north), Rome (277km/172 miles south) or another European city, then take a connecting flight or train. The flight from New York to Rome takes around nine hours; from the airport, take a shuttle train to Stazione Termini, then a train to Florence (2 hours).

ENTRY REQUIREMENTS

For the latest passport and visa information, look up the British embassy website at www.fco.gov.uk or the United States embassy at www.usembassy.gov. EU citizens do not require visas to visit Italy.

CUSTOMS REGULATIONS

● EU nationals do not have to declare goods imported for their personal use.
● The limits for non-EU visitors are 200 cigarettes or 100 small cigars or 250g of tobacco; 1 litre of alcohol (over 22 per cent alcohol) or 2 litres of fortified wine; 60ml of perfume.

AIRPORTS

You can choose from three airports—Galileo Galilei Airport at Pisa, the small Amerigo Vespucci Airport at Florence and Guglielmo Marconi Airport at Bologna. The flight takes approximately 2 hours from London.

120KM (75 MILES)

Florence Airport
4km (2.5 miles) to central Florence
Bus, 20 minutes
€5

Bologna Airport
105km (65 miles) to Florence
Bus then train, 1 hour, around €14.50

Pisa Airport
80km (50 miles) to Florence
Train, 1 hour 15 minutes
€5.70

FROM FLORENCE AIRPORT

Amerigo Vespucci Airport (☎ 055 306 1300; www.aeroporto.firenze.it), also known as La Peretola, is 4km (2.5 miles) northwest of the city. It handles mainly domestic flights, with a limited number of daily departures to other European cities. There are two terminal buildings. The airport is connected to the main station (Autostazione Sita) in Florence by the light blue Volainbus shuttle (administered by ATAF and SITA ☎ 800 424 500; www.ataf.net), which runs every 30 minutes from 6am to 8.30pm, then every hour until 11.30pm. The journey takes 20 minutes and tickets, which cost €4.50, can be bought on board. Taxis cost around €18, plus possible surcharges (always check and agree a price before you set off).

FROM PISA AIRPORT

Pisa's Galileo Galilei Airport (☎ 050 849 300; www.pisa-airport.com) is the region's main point of entry 80km (50 miles) west of Florence, but with good road and train connections to the city. The one spacious terminal handles domestic and European flights. Five trains a day leave the airport for Florence between 6.40am and around 10.20pm. The journey takes about 75 minutes and costs €5.70. Additional trains leave from Pisa Centrale station; a shuttle bus runs every 30 to 40 minutes from the airport to the main train station. Terravision (www.terravision.eu) runs an airport bus transfer, taking around 70 minutes, to Florence train station between 8.40am and 00.20am, costing €10 one way, €16 round-trip. A taxi to Florence could cost you more than €130. There is a helpful information office inside the terminal where you can buy tickets for trains and the bus.

FROM BOLOGNA AIRPORT
Guglielmo Marconi Airport (☎ 051 647 9615; www.bologna-airport.it) is 105km (65 miles) northeast of Florence in the Emilia-Romagna region and handles a large volume of European charter and scheduled flights, as well as budget airline flights. A shuttle bus costing about €5 takes passengers to Bologna Centrale station (www.grandistazione.it). From here the journey takes about an hour and costs around €10, depending on type of train taken. Make sure your ticket is valid for the right train. Rental cars are available in Terminal A. Taxis to Florence cost about €200.

ARRIVING BY TRAIN
The main station, Santa Maria Novella (www.grandistazione.it), has links with major Italian cities as well as Paris, Ostend and Frankfurt. Most buses in Florence depart from the station forecourt, and there are usually taxis waiting. Don't forget to validate your ticket, by inserting it into the orange box on the platform, before boarding your train.

ARRIVING BY LONG-DISTANCE BUS
Lazzi runs express services to and from Rome and links Florence with major European cities as part of the Eurolines network (✉ Piazza della Stazione 3r ☎ 055 363 041; www.lazzi.it).

TRAVEL INSURANCE

Take out your insurance as soon as you book your trip to ensure you are covered for delays. Most policies cover cancellation, medical expenses, accident compensation, personsal liability and loss of personal belongings (including money). Your policy should cover the cost of getting you home in case of medical emergency. An annual travel policy may be the best value if you intend to make several trips in a year away from home, but long trips abroad may not be covered. If you have private medical coverage, check your policy, as you may be covered while you are away.

CAR RENTAL

The major car rental groups are all represented in the region and have offices at airports, rail stations and in the bigger cities.

Getting Around

VISITORS WITH DISABILITIES

As in many other historic Italian cities, visitors with disabilities are far from well served in Florence, though things are improving. The official APT website (▷ 115) has detailed information for tourists with special needs. Many city museums are fully wheelchair-accessible, with ramps, elevators and appropriate bathrooms. The grey and green buses can take wheelchairs, as does the electric D bus, which goes through the heart of Florence (board via the electric platform at the rear door). Taxis do take wheelchairs but it is wise to let them know when you make a reservation.

The Tuscan capital has no metro or subway system, but the historic area is largely traffic-free and can be crossed on foot in 30 minutes. There are conventional bus services, but none of the routes are allowed to enter the traffic-free zone. These buses are useful, however, if you are staying on the outskirts of the city, or for getting around to the more outlying sights. In addition to the normal bus service there are four bus routes that do enter the traffic-free zone. Azienda Trasporti Area Fiorentina (ATAF) is responsible for public transportation in Florence (www.ataf.net).

BUSES
Bus routes in Florence are numbered and many start and end at the railway station at regular intervals. The zippy little electric buses that run through the traffic-free zone, identified by letters (A–D), link all kinds of places in the narrow streets of the old city. Buy tickets at bars, tobacconists and from the ATAF booth on Piazza Stazione before boarding. Once on board, insert your ticket into the small orange box and it will be stamped with the time. Failure to validate your ticket can result in a hefty fine. The ticket is valid for the next 90 minutes for any bus; cost €1.20 or €2 if purchased on board. A multiple ticket gives you four 90-minute tickets; cost €4.50. The tourist information office by the station has bus maps.

HOP-ON-HOP-OFF BUS
If you really want to avoid any leg work, or want an overview of how the city is laid out, take an open-top bus ride with City Sightseeing (☎ 055 290 451; www.city-sightseeing.it). This bus permits visitors to get on and off at any number of designated stops on the tourist itinerary. The ticket is valid for 24 hours and costs €22.

LONG-DISTANCE BUS
There are three main bus companies in Florence: **Lazzi** ✉ Piazza della Stazione 47 ☎ 055 363 041; www.lazzi.it

SITA serves the south and east region ✉ Via Santa Caterina da Siena 15r ☎ 800 373760 (in Italy only); www.sitabus.it (in Italian only).
CAP serves the region to the northeast of Florence, the Mugello ✉ Largo Fratelli Alinari 9 ☎ 055 214 637; www.capautolinee.it

TAXIS
The official white Florentine taxis are comfortable and clean. You can hail them from central places such as the station or Piazza del Duomo, or call one of the official cab companies: Radio Taxi SO.CO.TA. (☎ 055 4798/4242) or Radio Taxi CO.TA.FI. (☎ 055 4390). The meter starts running the moment your call is received. Supplements are charged for baggage and for journeys at night.

BICYCLES AND MOTORCYCLES
Bicycles can be rented from Florence by Bike ✉ Via San Zanobi 120–122r ☎ 055 488 992 Mopeds and motorcycles can be rented from Alinari ✉ Via Zanobi 38r ☎ 055 280 500

CARS
It is really not worth driving around Florence. Much of the city is closed to traffic, there is a one-way system and parking is difficult. However, a car is ideal if you plan to tour the surrounding Tuscan countryside. If you do rent a car, try to book a hotel with parking. Main car rental companies are:
Avis ✉ Borgo Ognissanti 128r ☎ 055 213 629
Europcar ✉ Borgo Ognissanti 53–55r ☎ 055 290 438
Hertz Italiana ✉ Via Finiguerra 33r ☎ 055 239 8205
Tuscany's road system ranges from motorways (expressways) to winding lanes, and driving around outside the city is easy and a pleasure. Tolls are payable on highways (*autostrade*) and most fuel stations in the country now take credit cards, but by no means all.
Highway emergency/Breakdown service (ACI): ☎ 803 116

TIPS

● You should board a bus through the front or rear door, but exit through the middle ones.
● Children travel free if they are less than 1m (3ft 3in) in height. Their height is checked against the box that you validate your ticket in.
● Smoking is not allowed on buses.
● Most buses are adapted for people with disabilities.
● Bus routes are not always the same on the return leg so check the map at the bus stop to be sure you can get off at the stop of your choice.

OTHER TRANSPORTATION

● A environmentally friendly and novel way of getting around central Florence is to rent a Segway, a silent, two-wheeled self-balancing electric vehicle (☎ 055 239 885; www.segwayfirenze.com).
● Hail a pedicab or bicycle rickshaw—with room enough for two adults or one adult and two children (www.pedicabfirenze.it).
● Horse-drawn carriages known as *fiaccere* offer hour-long city tours and depart from various venues. These have the bonus of being able to be enter small pedestrian streets. (Check with the tourist office.)

Essential Facts

PRESS

● The Florentines preferred newspaper is *La Nazione*, a national paper produced in Florence.
● You can buy foreign newspapers and magazines at the station and at Sorbi, the kiosk in Piazza della Signoria.

MONEY

The euro is the official currency of Italy. Bank notes come in denominations of 5, 10, 20, 50, 100, 200 and 500 euros and coins in denominations of 1, 2, 5, 10, 20 and 50 cents and 1 and 2 euros

10 euros

50 euros

200 euros

500 euros

ELECTRICITY
● Voltage is 220 volts and sockets take two round pins.

EMERGENCY TELEPHONE NUMBERS
● Police ☎ 113; 112 (Carabinieri)
● Fire ☎ 115
● Ambulance ☎ 118
● State Police headquarters ✉ Via Zara 2 ☎ 055 49771

LOST PROPERTY
● Lost property office ✉ Via Veracini 5 ☎ 055 334 802 🕘 9–12; closed Sun, Thu.
● Report losses of passports to the police and other items to the Questura at Via Zara 2 ☎ 055 49771
● Lost property office at the station ✉ Stazione Santa Maria Novella ☎ 055 235 6120 🕘 Daily 4.15am–1.30am

MAIL
● Main post office ✉ Via Pellicceria 3 ☎ 055 273 6481 🕘 Mon–Sat 8.15–7; www.poste.it
● There is another big post office at ✉ Via Pietrapiana 53–55 ☎ 055 267 421 🕘 Mon–Fri 8.15–7, Sat 8.15–12.30.
● Stamps (*francobolli*) can be purchased from post offices or from tobacconists displaying a white T sign on a black or blue background.
● Post boxes are small, red and marked *Poste* or *Lettere*. The slot on the left is for addresses within the city and the slot on the right is for other destinations.

MEDICINES AND MEDICAL TREATMENT
● EU nationals receive reduced cost medical treatment on production of the relevant document (EHIC card for Britons). Private medical insurance for UK and all other nationals is still advised.
● Medical emergencies ☎ 118
● Tourist medical service: has English-speaking doctors also available for call-outs ✉ Via Lorenzo il Magnifico 59 ☎ 055 475 411

⊕ Mon–Fri 11am–midnight, 5–6,
Sat 11am–midnight; no appointment needed.
● Hospital: Santa Maria Nuova ✉ Piazza Santa
Maria Nuova 1 ☎ 055 27581.
Interpreters can be arranged free through
Ospedale di Careggi (surgical accident and
emergency unit) ✉ Viale Pieraccini 17 ☎ 055
794 9644; also dental services ☎ 055 794
7401 **⊕** Mon–Sat 8.30–12.30
● Pharmacies are indicated by a large green or
red cross. For pharmacy information ☎ 800
420 707 (toll-free from within Italy).
● All-night pharmacies:
Comunale 13 della Stazione ✉ At train station
☎ 055 216 761;
All'insegna del Moro-Taverna ✉ Piazza San
Giovanni 20r ☎ 055 211 343;
Molteni ✉ Via dei Calzaiuoli 7r ☎ 055 289
490

MONEY AND CREDIT CARDS
● Credit cards are widely accepted.
● ATMs are now plentiful.

NATIONAL HOLIDAYS
● 1 Jan: New Year's Day; 6 Jan: Epiphany;
Easter Sunday; Easter Monday; 25 Apr:
Liberation Day; 1 May: Labour Day; 15 Aug:
Assumption; 1 Nov: All Saints' Day; 8 Dec:
Immaculate Conception; 25 Dec: Christmas
Day; 26 Dec: St. Stephen's Day.

TOILETS
● Italian toilets are generally improving both in cleanliness and facilities.
● Expect to pay about €0.60 for toilets. Those away from the main tourist areas are usually free.
● A new service of 22 public toilets has been opened in Piazza San Giovanni near the Baptistery.
● Most bars and cafes have toilets, which usually allow anybody to use them (although it's polite to have at least a drink).
● Florence has promoted the initiative 'Courtesy Point' in which several bars and cafes have made their toilets available to the public.

CONSULATES	
British Consulate	✉ Lungarno Corsini 2 ☎ 055 284 133
US Consulate	✉ Lungarno Amerigo Vespucci 38 ☎ 055 266 951

PLACES OF WORSHIP	
Anglican	St. Mark's ✉ Via Maggio 16–18 ☎ 055 294 764
American Episcopal Church	St. James' ✉ Via Rucellai 9 ☎ 055 294 417
Lutheran	✉ Lungarno Torrigiani 11 ☎ 055 234 2775
Synagogue	✉ Via Farini 4 ☎ 055 245 252
Russian Orthodox	✉ Via Leone X 8 ☎ 055 490 148
Mosque	✉ Via Borgo Allegri 64–66r

ETIQUETTE

● Make the effort to speak some Italian: It will be appreciated.
● Shake hands on introduction and on leaving; once you know people better you can replace this with a kiss on each cheek.
● Use the polite form, *lei*, unless the other person uses *tu*.
● Always say *buon giorno* (hello) and *arrivederci* (goodbye) in shops.
● Italians do not get drunk in public.
● Smoking is banned in enclosed public places.

PRECAUTIONS

● Take care of wallets, handbags and backpacks as pickpockets target tourists.
● Keep the receipts and numbers of your traveller's cheques separately from the traveller's cheques.
● Keep a copy of the front page of your passport.
● List the numbers and expiration dates of your credit cards and keep the list separately.
● If a theft occurs, make a statement (*denuncia*) at a police station within 24 hours if you wish to make an insurance claim.
● After dark avoid Le Cascine and the station.

OPENING TIMES

● Banks: generally 8.30–3; in some instances also 2.45–4 Mon–Fri.
● Post offices: Mon–Fri 8.15–1.30 Sat 8.15–12.30.
● Shops: normally 8.30–1 and from 3 or 4 until 7 or 8; or 10–7.
● Museums: see individual entries.
● Churches: 7 or 8–12.30 and then from between 3 and 4 until 7.30. Main tourist attractions often stay open longer. No two are the same.

TELEPHONES

● Public phones are silver and orange. There is a phone centre known as Il Cairo, which includes internet access ☒ Via de' Macci 90r ☎ 055 263 8336 🕒 Mon–Sat 9.30–9, Sun 3–7.
● Few public telephones take coins. Phone cards (*carta* or *scheda* or *tessera telefonica*) are the most practical way to use a public phone.
● Directory Enquiries ☎ 1254
● International directory enquiries ☎ 176 International operator ☎ 170; you can also make reverse charge international calls on this number via the operator.
● Cheap rate is all day Sunday and 9pm–8am (national) on other days; 10pm–8am (international).
● To call Italy from the UK, dial 00 followed by 39 (the code for Italy) then the number. To call the UK from Italy dial 00 44 then drop the first zero from the area code.
● To call Italy from the US dial 011 followed by 39. To call the US from Italy dial 00 1.
● Florence's area code (055) must always be dialled even if you are calling from within Florence.

TOURIST INFORMATION OFFICE

● Principal tourist office ☒ Via Cavour 1r ☎ 055 290 832/3; fax 055 276 0383; www.firenzeturismo.it

Language

Italian pronunciation is totally consistent. Cs and gs are hard when they are followed by an *a*, *o* or *u* (as in 'cat' and 'got'), and soft if followed by an *e* or an *i* (as in 'child' or 'geranium').

The Tuscans often pronounce their *cs* and *chs* as *hs*.

USEFUL WORDS AND PHRASES

buon giorno	good morning
buona sera	good afternoon/ evening
buona notte	good night
ciao	hello/ good-bye (informal)
arrivederci	good-bye (informal)
arrivederla	good-bye (formal)
per favore	please
grazie	thank you
prego	you're welcome
come sta/stai?	how are you?
sto bene	I'm fine
mi dispiace	I'm sorry
scusi/scusa	excuse me/ I beg your pardon
permesso	excuse me (in a crowd)
quant'è?	how much is it?
quando?	when?
avete...?	do you have ...?
qui/qua	here

BASIC VOCABULARY

sì	yes
no	no
non ho capito	I do not understand
sinistra	left
destra	right
entrata	entrance
uscita	exit
aperto	open
chiuso	closed
buono	good
cattivo	bad
grande	big
piccolo	small
con	with
senza	without
più	more

NUMBERS

uno/primo	1/first
due/secondo	2/second
tre/terzo	3/third
quattro/ quarto	4/fourth
cinque/quinto	5/fifth
sei	6
sette	7
otto	8
nove	9
dieci	10
venti	20
cinquanta	50
cento	100
mille	1,000
milione	1,000,000

EMERGENCIES

aiuto!	help!
dov'è il telefono più vicino?	where is the nearest telephone?
c'è stato un incidente	there has been an accident
chiamate la polizia	call the police
chiamate un medico/ un'ambulanza	call a doctor/an ambulance
pronto soccorso	first aid
dov'è l'ospedale più vicino?	where is the nearest hospital?

123

Timeline

THE FLORIN

Florence minted its own coins, florins, in silver in 1235 and in gold in 1252. Soon they were being used as the standard coin in Europe, evidence of the pre-eminence of Florence in European finance.

BEFORE 1000

Florence started to grow in 59BC as a result of an agrarian law passed by Julius Caesar, granting land to retired army veterans. Byzantine walls were added to the Roman walls in AD541–44, as protection against the Ostrogoths. The Lombards took Tuscany in 570 but were defeated in the early 9th century by Charlemagne. Florence then became part of the Holy Roman Empire, ruled by imperial princes known as Margraves.

1115 The first comune (city state) is formed. Florence is run by a 100-strong assembly.

1250–60 The Primo Popolo regime controls Florence, dominated by trade guilds.

1296 The building of the Duomo begins, under Arnolfo di Cambio.

1340s Florence faces economic crisis after Edward III of England bankrupts the Peruzzi and Bardi and the Black Death plague halves the population.

1378 The uprising of the *ciompi* (wool carders) is the high point of worker unrest.

1406 Florence captures Pisa, gaining direct access to the sea.

1458 Cosimo de' Medici is recognized as ruler of Florence.

1469–92 Lorenzo the Magnificent rules.

1494 Florence surrenders to Charles VIII of France. Savonarola, a zealous monk, takes control of the city.

1498 Savonarola is burned at the stake after four years of rule, and Florence becomes a republic.

1502 The Republic of Florence retakes Pisa.

1570 Cosimo I creates a Tuscan state free from the Holy Roman Empire.

1743 Anna Maria Luisa, last of the Medici, dies. Florence is then ruled by the house of Lorraine under Francis Stephen.

1799–1814 Tuscany is occupied by Napoleon's troops.

1865–70 Florence becomes the capital of Italy. King Vittorio Emanuele is installed in the Pitti Palace.

1944 On 4 August, Germans blow up all the bridges in Florence with the exception of the Ponte Vecchio.

1966 The River Arno bursts its banks: Florence is flooded, the waters reaching to more than 6.5m (22 feet) in some areas.

1993 The Uffizi Gallery is bombed.

2004 Michelangelo's *David* is unveiled in the Galleria dell'Accademia after controversial restoration.

2006 Florence Airport (Amerigo Vespucci) reopens in April after major renovation work.

2009 Matteo Renzi is elected as Florence's mayor. His fresh approach begins to bring improvements in facilities for residents and visitors alike.

FAMOUS FLORENTINES

The poet Dante Alighieri, author of the *Divine Comedy*, was born in Florence in 1265. He was exiled from the city in 1302 because of his sympathies with the White Guelphs, and died in 1321.

Michelangelo Buonarroti (1475–1564) created some of his most famous works in Florence, including the sculpture *David*. Born in Caprese, he was buried in Florence's Santa Croce.

Political philosopher Niccolò Machiavelli was born in Florence in 1469.

Galileo Galilei (1564–1642), from Pisa, spent much of his life in Florence as the Medici court mathematician.

From far left: Bust of Cosimo di Giovanni de' Medici and on his horse; Napoleon Bonaparte; Dante Alighieri; fleur-de-lys guild emblem; the defensive Forte di Belvedere

Index

Florence's
25 BEST

WRITTEN BY Susannah Perry
ADDITIONAL WRITING Jackie Staddon and Hilary Weston
UPDATED BY Jackie Staddon and Hilary Weston
DESIGN WORK Jacqueline Bailey
COVER DESIGN Tigist Getachew
INDEXER Marie Lorimer
IMAGE RETOUCHING AND REPRO Sarah Montgomery and James Tims
REVIEWING EDITOR Linda Schmidt
PROJECT EDITOR Bookwork Creative Associates Ltd
SERIES EDITOR Marie-Claire Jefferies

ISBN 978-1-4000-0543-7

EIGHTH EDITION

IMPORTANT TIP
Time inevitably brings changes, so always confirm prices, travel facts, and other perishable information when it matters. Although Fodor's cannot accept responsibility for errors, you can use this guide in the confidence that we have taken every care to ensure its accuracy.

SPECIAL SALES
This book is available for special discounts for bulk purchases for sales promotions or premiums. Special editions, including personalized covers, excerpts of existing books, and corporate imprints, can be created in large quantities for special needs. For more information, write to Special Markets/Premium Sales, 1745 Broadway, 3–2, New York, NY 10019 or email specialmarkets@randomhouse.com.

Color separation by AA Digital Department
Printed and bound by Leo Paper Products, China
10 9 8 7 6 5 4 3 2

A04803
Maps in this title produced from mapping © MAIRDUMONT / Falk Verlag 2011
Transport map © Communicarta Ltd, UK

The Automobile Association would like to thank the following photographers and companies for their assistance in the preparation of this book.

Abbreviations for the picture credits are as follows – (t) top; (b) bottom; (c) centre; (l) left; (r) right; (AA) AA World Travel Library

1 AA/Simon McBrideAA J Tims; 2–18t AA/Simon McBride; 4cl AA/Simon McBride; 5c AA/Ken Paterson; 6cl AA/Simon McBride; 6cc AA/Clive Sawyer; 6cr AA/Simon McBride; 6bl AA/Terry Harris; 6bc AA/Ken Paterson; 6br AA/Simon McBride; 7cl AA/J Edmanson; 7cr AA/Simon McBride; 7bl AA/Clive Sawyer; 7br AA/Simon McBride; 10ctr AA/Simon McBride; 10cr AA/Simon McBride; 10cbr AA/Terry Harris; 10br AA/Simon McBrideAA J Tims; 11ctl AA/Terry Harris; 11cbl AA/Ken Paterson; 11bl AA/Clive SawyerAA J Tims; 13ctl AA/Clive Sawyer; 13cl AA/Terry Harris; 13cbl AA/Clive Sawyer; 13bl AA/Terry Harris; 14ctr AA/Max JourdanAA J Tims; 14cr AA/Simon McBride; 14cbr AA/Ken Paterson; 14br AA/Terry Harris; 16ctr AA/Simon McBride; 16cbr AA/Ken Paterson; 16br AA/Simon McBride; 17ctl AA/Simon McBride; 17cl AA/Simon McBride; 17cbl AA/Clare Garcia; 17bl AA/Terry Harris; 18ctr AA/Clive Sawyer; 18cr Photodisc; 18cbr AA/Clive Sawyer; 18br AA/Clive Sawyer; 19t AA/Simon McBride; 19ct AA/Ken Paterson; 19cb AA/Richard Ireland; 19b AA/Terry Harris; 20/21 AA/Clive Sawyer; 24l AA/Clive Sawyer; 24/25t AA/Clive Sawyer; 24/25c AA/Simon McBride; 25tr AA/J Edmanson; 25cl AA/Ken Paterson; 25c AA/Ken Paterson; 25cr AA/Ken Paterson; 26l AA/Simon McBride; 26r Santa Croce, Florence, Giraudon/Bridgeman Art Library; 27l AA/Clive Sawyer; 27r Scala, Florence 2006; 28l AA/Simon McBride; 28c AA/Simon McBride; 28r AA/Simon McBride; 29l AA/Simon McBride; 29r AA/Clive Sawyer; 30tl AA; 30/31t AA/Simon McBride; 30c AA/Simon McBride; 30/31c AA/Terry Harris; 31tr AA/Simon McBride; 31cr AA/Simon McBride; 32l AA/Clive SawyerAA J Tims; 32c AA/Barrie SmithAA J Tims; 32r AA/J Edmanson; 33 AA/Simon McBride; 34t AA/Simon McBride; 34cl AA/Terry Harris; 34c AA/Clive Sawyer; 34cr AA/Clive Sawyer; 35 AA/Terry Harris; 36l AA/Clive SawyerAA J Tims; 36c AA/Terry Harris; 36r AA/Clive SawyerAA J Tims; 37-39t AA/Ken Paterson; 37bl AA/Ken Paterson; 37br AA/Clive Sawyer; 38bl AA/Clive Sawyer; 38br AA/Clive Sawyer; 39bl AA/Simon McBride; 39br AA/Clive Sawyer; 40 AA/Terry Harris; 41t AA/Simon McBride; 42t AA/Simon McBride; 43t AA/Simon McBride; 44t AA/Simon McBride; 45 AA/Terry Harris; 46t AA/Terry Harris; 47t AA/Eric Meacher; 48t AA/Simon McBride; 49t AA/Clive Sawyer; 50t AA/Ken Paterson; 51 AA/Simon McBride; 54 AA/Clive Sawyer; 55 AA/Simon McBride; 56l AA/Simon McBride; 56c AA/Simon McBride; 56r AA/Ken Paterson; 57l AA/Terry Harris; 57r AA/Terry Harris; 58tl AA/Simon McBride; 58tr AA/Clive Sawyer; 58cl AA/Ken Paterson; 58cr AA/Simon McBride; 59t AA/Simon McBride; 59cl AA/Simon McBride; 59cr AA/J Edmanson; 60 Galleria dell' Accademia, Florence/Bridgeman Art Library; 60/61 Raffaello Bencini/Alinari Archives, Florence; 61r AA/Simon McBride; 62l AA/Simon McBride; 62r AA/Simon McBrideAA J Tims; 63l AA/Simon McBride; 63r AA/Simon McBride; 64l AA/Terry Harris; 64r AA/Terry Harris; 65l AA/Simon McBride; 65r AA/Simon McBride; 66l AA/Simon McBride; 66c AA/Clive Sawyer; 66r AA/J Edmanson; 67l AA/Clive Sawyer; 67r AA/Terry Harris; 68-69t AA/Ken Paterson; 68b AA/Simon McBride; 69bl AA/Terry Harris; 69br AA/Terry Harris AA/C Sawyer; 70t AA/Terry Harris; 71t AA/Terry Harris; 72t AA/Simon McBride; 73t AA/Simon McBride; 74t Digitalvision; 75t AA/Simon McBride; 76t AA/Terry Harris; 77 AA/Clive Sawyer; 80 AA/Simon McBrideAA J Tims; 81 AA/Simon McBride; 82l AA/Ken Paterson; 82r AA/Clive Sawyer; 83l AA/Clive Sawyer; 83r AA/Simon McBride; 84t AA/Simon McBride; 84c AA J Tims AA/Richard Ireland; 84/85 AA/J Edmanson; 86-87t AA/Ken Paterson; 86bl AA/Simon McBride; 86br AA/Clive Sawyer; 87b AA/Simon McBride; 88t AA/Terry Harris; 89t AA/Ken Paterson; 90t AA/Simon McBride; 91t AA/Digitalvision; 91c AA/Terry Harris; 92t AA/Terry Harris; 93 AA/Terry Harris; 96 AA/J TimsSeat Archive/Alinari Archives; 97l Il Gioco del Ponte dei Pisani, Italian School, 17th century, Museo Stibbert, Florence/Bridgeman Art Library/AA/C Sawyer; 97r AA/T Harris; 98t AA/Ken Paterson; 98b AA/Clive Sawyer; 99t AA/Ken Paterson; 99bl AA/Terry Harris; 99br AA/Terry Harris; 100t AA/Ken Paterson; 100b AA/Terry Harris; 101t AA/Simon McBride; 102t AA/Michelle Chaplow; 103t Digitalvision; 104t Photodisc; 105t AA/Clive Sawyer; 106t David Wasserman/brandxpictures; 107 AA/Clive Sawyer; 108-112t AA/Clive Sawyer; 108ctr AA/J Edmanson; 108cr AA/Clive Sawyer; 108cbr AA/Simon McBride; 108br AA/Terry Harris; 113 AA/Terry Harris; 114-125t AA/Terry Harris; 118b AA/J Tims AA/Terry Harris; 120 ECB; 124bl AA; 124bc AA/Clive Sawyer; |124bc AA; 124br AA/Clive Sawyer; 125bl AA/Clive Sawyer; 125br AA/Simon McBride.

Every effort has been made to trace the copyright holders, and we apologise in advance for any accidental errors. We would be happy to apply the corrections in the following edition of this publication.